H.E.L.P.

Home Emergency Ladies' Pal

Published by

XYZYX

INFORMATION CORPORATION

21116 Vanowen Street
Canoga Park, Calif. 91303

First Edition
Printed in U.S.A.
First Printing November 1972

Library of Congress Catalog Card Number: 72-92788

1001172

This book is printed on 70% recycled paper. Join us in
the reclaiming of waste material to reduce pollution and
conserve America's natural resources.

H.E.L.P. stands for Home Emergency Ladies' Pal.

With a copy of it in your home you're equipped to handle, on your own, a whole range of home emergencies, and to deal with them before they become out-of-control emergencies. It is, in effect, a "family doctor" for the equipment that you use every day in your home.

You know that the modern conveniences which bring comfort and ease into our lives can also bring complications and confusion — especially when they go wrong.

H.E.L.P. ends the complications and confusion.

It is based on the principle that even the most complicated jobs become simple, if properly broken down into small steps. That basic principle and its use in H.E.L.P. can save your nerves, your time and cut your repair bills.

Every operation described in H.E.L.P. has been analyzed and reduced to a series of step-by-step instructions.

The instructions are written in a controlled language form which you will understand easily.

These are supported by illustration patterns which lead you through the steps to be taken.

H.E.L.P. works.

With the aid of a number of American housewives H.E.L.P. has been tested and proven to be an extremely valuable new home-help idea.

People just like you handled complex repair jobs expertly and efficiently using H.E.L.P. So if you've ever felt at the mercy of today's modern conveniences . . .

Relax.

H.E.L.P. is here.

HOW TO USE THIS BOOK

This book is arranged so you can find things fast and easily — as it should be, to be of help in emergencies. Run your finger down the Table of Contents (opposite) and find the general section covering your problem (for example, if you have a drain problem, your finger would stop at PLUMBING). Now turn the book to look at the right edge and "fan out" the pages to see where the black line in the Table of Contents picks up again in the book. In this way you can turn directly to Plumbing on Page 37.

Do not pick up the book and attempt to read it for enjoyment, as you might other books. This book is not designed to entertain you. In some places it is deliberately repetitious. But these aspects spring from the fact that it is a tool designed to do a job — namely, help you in emergencies.

Some of the procedures may be confusing if you start reading in the middle. Therefore, when you set out to do any of the jobs covered in this book, always start at the beginning of the appropriate section or subsection. Scan through first, and then begin step by step. If you do this, you won't get confused!

Most pages consist of words on the left and illustrations on the right. Any part referred to by name is followed by a number in parentheses — for example, valve [4]. This part is found in the illustration by looking for the same number (4, in this case) and noting where the arrow points. This way you always know what is being referred to, where it is and what it looks like. Sometimes the picture will not look exactly the same as the item in your house, because of the great variety of hardware on the market. But we have covered all of the more common types.

A word is needed about CAUTIONS and WARNINGS. Occasionally there is a chance you will damage something if you are not careful. We call your attention to this by a CAUTION before the step is performed. If there is the possibility of injuring somebody, we use a WARNING.

The Emergency Medical Aid section is unique in that there is really no substitute for on-the-spot judgment in medical emergencies. We have given generally accepted procedures for treating common accidents. These should be considered as guidelines only, which will help you avoid hasty, unthinking actions and indicate what can be done until professional care can be obtained.

Table of Contents

EMERGENCY HOME SUPPLIES

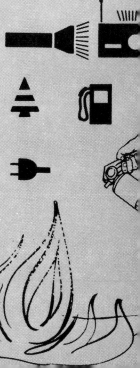

EMERGENCY HOME SUPPLIES

The following items should be kept readily available in a central location and in good condition in case of emergencies.

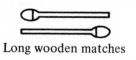
Long wooden matches

Use for lighting candles and relighting pilots on gas appliances. Be sure matches are kept in metal container out of sight and reach of children.

Flashlight

Keep it handy. Check it frequently for proper operation. Keep extra batteries available.

Baking soda

Keep near cooking area at all times to put out grease or flammable liquid fires.

Candles
(Bowl-type)

Keep handy in case of power failure. Bowl will help prevent fire in case candle is overturned.

Portable radio
(battery operated)

Use for receiving broadcast instructions in case of widespread power failure. Keep extra batteries available.

EMERGENCY HOME SUPPLIES

 Keep connected to water outlet at all times for emergency use in case of fire. Be sure hose will reach all areas of home.

Garden hose and nozzle

 Be sure you know how to use your extinguisher. Check it regularly. DO NOT let it give you a false sense of security. Page 4.

Fire extinguisher (ABC type)

 Keep several spare fuses next to your fuse box. Number on end of fuse indicates size. When replacing blown fuses, BE SURE number on end of the new fuse is the same as number on old fuse.

Fuses (if your home has a fuse box)

 Only a few items are required to treat most common home injuries and discomforts. Be sure they are readily available. Page 5.

First Aid Supplies

EMERGENCY HOME SUPPLIES

Fire Extinguisher.

Fires are divided into three types:

 Type A fires: ordinary combustibles, such as wood, paper, etc.

 Type B fires: flammable liquids, such as cooking grease, gasoline, etc.

 Type C fires: electrical

Fire extinguishers are manufactured to combat one or more types of fires.

An ABC rated fire extinguisher is the best for general home use. It can be used for all types of household fires.

When you buy a fire extinguisher, carefully read the instructions that come with the extinguisher so that you will be able to use it properly in an emergency.

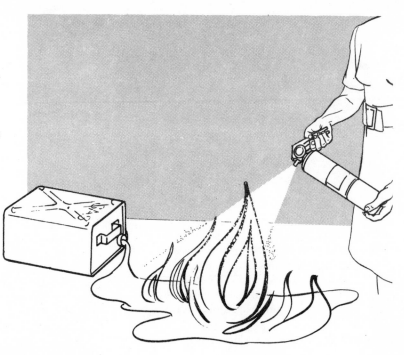

4

EMERGENCY HOME SUPPLIES

First Aid Supplies

First aid supplies for treating most minor injuries likely to happen in a home are neither complicated nor expensive.

Keep the following supplies readily available in your medicine cabinet for treating minor injuries and discomforts.

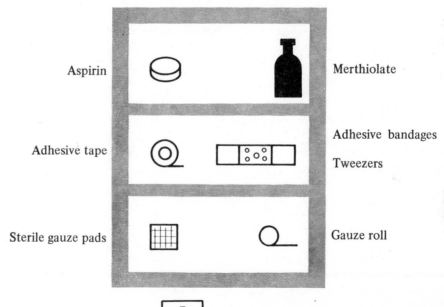

Aspirin

Merthiolate

Adhesive tape

Adhesive bandages

Tweezers

Sterile gauze pads

Gauze roll

5

EMERGENCY HOME SUPPLIES

Useful Tools

Tools required for emergency home repairs are common and inexpensive.

The following tools are useful in performing most emergency repairs around the home. You should be familiar with their names and uses.

Channellock pliers [1]
Pipe wrench [2]
Common screwdriver [3]
Phillips screwdriver [4]
Diagonal cutting pliers [5]
Knife [6]
Paint brush [7]
Claw hammer [8]
Adjustable wrench [9]

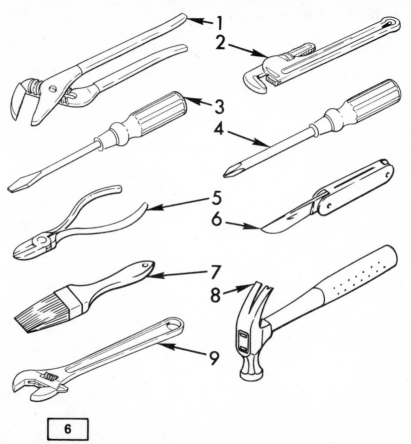

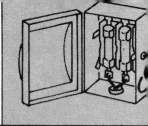

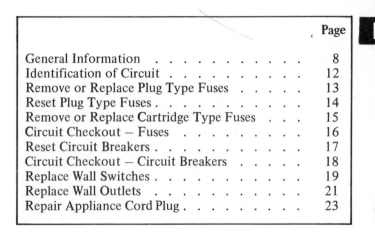

ELECTRICAL

Plug in fuse (3 types)

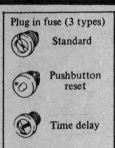

Standard

Pushbutton reset

Time delay

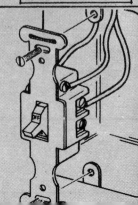

ELECTRICAL

General Information

- Electrical power comes to your home from the power company.

- This power flows through your meter [1] which records how much electricity you use.

- The power flows to a main power control switch [3], located in your fuse or circuit breaker box [2].

- When the main switch is turned on, electrical current flows to each fuse or circuit breaker [4].

- Each fuse or circuit breaker [4] controls the distribution of electricity to wall switches and outlets in different areas of your home. These different areas are called circuits [5].

- Each circuit may have a number of wall switches and outlets within it.

- Fuses and circuit breakers [4] and circuits [5] will be your primary concern as you encounter electrical problems.

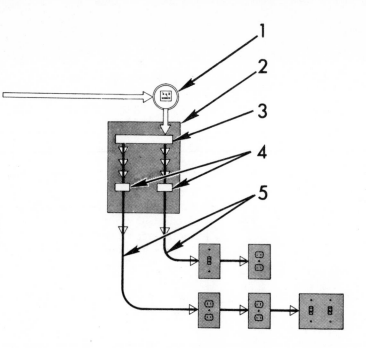

- Fuse and circuit breaker boxes differ in appearance. They can be located indoors or outdoors. Generally they will be found near your meter.

ELECTRICAL

Fuse and Circuit Breaker Boxes

- Indoor — probable locations are basement, garage or utility room.
- Outdoor — probable locations are back or side of house.

Fuse or Circuit Breaker Boxes	Cover Open	Main Switch	Fuse-Circuit Breaker	Remove — Replace — Reset
	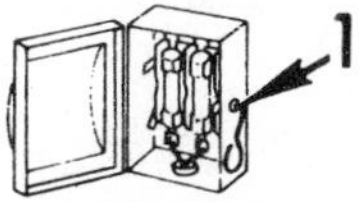	Handle [1] moves up and down.	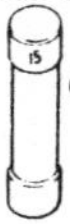 Cartridge fuse	Page ___15___
	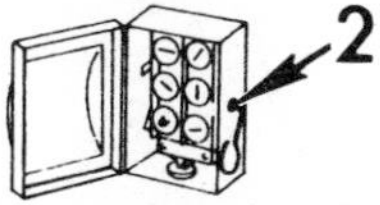	Handle [2] moves up and down.	Plug in fuse (3 types)  Standard  Time delay	Page ___13___
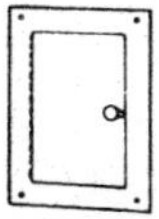	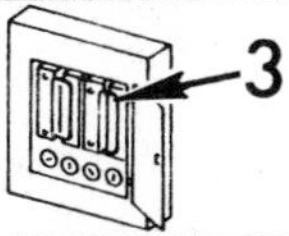	Switch [3] marked "Main" pulls out and pushes in.	 Pushbutton reset	Page ___14___
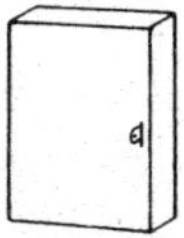	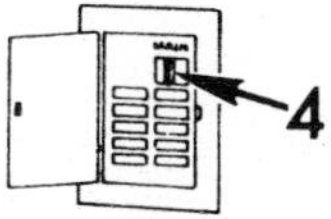	Large switch [4] pushes in and out or moves side to side.	Circuit breakers (2 types)  Toggle type	Page ___17___
		Large switch [5] pushes in and out or moves side to side.	 Pushbutton type	

The left column of the chart shows the most common fuse or circuit breaker boxes. The other columns show what is inside the box. Check the box in your home.

ELECTRICAL

General Information

Draw the floor plan of your home in the space provided on next page. If space provided is not large enough for your home, draw on a separate piece of paper and tape information to floor plan page. Locate the following items and sketch them into the floor plan:

- Fuse box [1], or circuit breaker box [4]

- Electrical outlets [5] in each room

- Wall switches [6] in each room

In your sketch, use numbers or colored pencils to identify the circuit controlled by each fuse [2] or circuit breaker [3].

The steps on Page 12 will aid you in identifying each circuit.

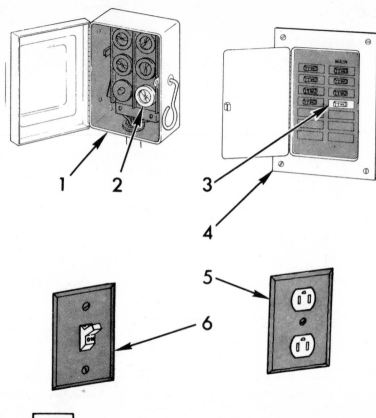

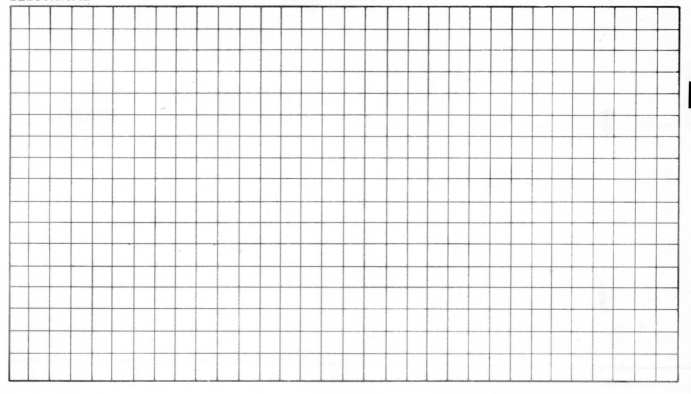

ELECTRICAL

Identification of Circuit

Each outlet or appliance that does not have electricity when a fuse is removed or circuit breaker is OFF, is in the circuit controlled by that fuse or circuit breaker.

When identifying circuits, do not place MAIN circuit breaker [3] to OFF.

Removal of plug type fuses [8] is explained on Page 13.

Removal of cartridge type fuses [6] is explained on Page 15.

1. Place one circuit breaker [5] to OFF or remove one fuse [6,8].

2. Place all wall switches [1] to ON.

3. Using a radio or small lamp, check each outlet [2] for electricity.

All major appliances such as electric range and washing machine are usually on separate circuits.

4. Turn all major appliances ON and OFF.

Place a label in door of box [4,7] opposite removed fuse [6,8] or tripped circuit breaker [5] identifying each outlet or appliance that did not have electricity applied.

5. Place circuit breaker [5] to on or install fuse [6,8].

6. Repeat Steps 1 through 5 for all circuit breakers or fuses.

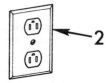

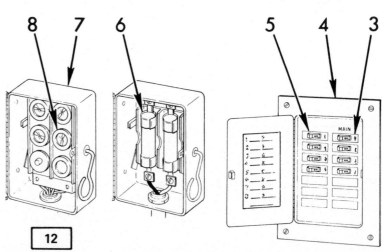

12

ELECTRICAL

Remove or Replace Plug Type Fuses

WARNING

You can be seriously injured by electricity. Do not touch any wires. If ground or floor is damp, place boards over the area and stand on boards when removing or replacing fuses.

1. Open fuse box cover. If your fuses are type [1] complete Steps 2 through 6. If your fuses are reset type [3] go to Page 14.

If glass window [2] on any fuse [1] is blackened, a short circuit caused your fuse to blow. Go to Step 2.

If no window is blackened, continue on.

Look for melted wire [5] or loose spring end [4] inside glass window [2]. Fuse in this condition must be replaced.

Refer to your circuit sketch or label inside fuse box cover for switches and outlets controlled by blown fuse.

2. Place all wall switches to OFF. Remove electrical plugs from all outlets in this circuit.

3. Remove blown fuse [1] by turning counter-clockwise.

Number on end of fuse [1,3] indicates size of fuse. When replacing blown fuses, BE SURE number on new fuse is the same as number on old fuse.

4. Install fuse [1] in socket. Tighten fuse by turning clockwise.

5. Close fuse box cover.

6. Go to Page 16 for circuit checkout.

ELECTRICAL

Reset Plug Type Fuses

Reset buttons [3] on fuses [2] pop out, or trip to break circuit when overloaded.

1. Open fuse box cover [1].

2. Check buttons on fuses [2]. Locate button that has tripped.

Refer to your circuit sketch or label inside fuse box cover [1] for switches and outlets controlled by fuse [2].

3. Place all wall switches to OFF. Remove electrical plugs from all outlets in this circuit.

4. Push in fuse button [3]. Close fuse box cover [1]. Go to Page 16 for circuit checkout.

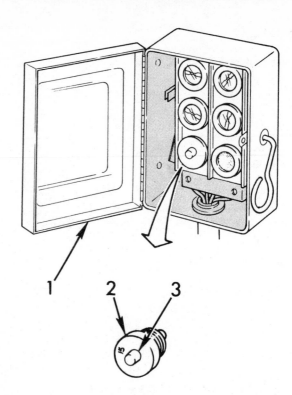

ELECTRICAL

Remove or Replace Cartridge Type Fuses

WARNING

You can be seriously injured by electricity. Do not touch any wires. If ground or floor is damp, place boards over the area and stand on boards when removing or replacing fuses.

1.   Place main switch [4] to OFF.
     Open fuse box cover [5].

Refer to your circuit sketch or label inside fuse box cover for switches and outlets controlled by blown fuse.

2.   Locate blown fuse [2].

3.   Place all switches to OFF. Remove electrical plugs from all outlets in this circuit.

WARNING

Metal end caps [1] may be hot. When removing fuse let fuse fall to floor or ground.

4.   Using a wooden stick, pry blown fuse from holder [3].

Number on fuse [2] indicates size of fuse. When replacing blown fuse, BE SURE number on new fuse is the same as number on old fuse.

5.   Press new fuse into holder [3]. Close fuse box door. Place main switch [4] to ON.

6.   Go to next page for circuit checkout.

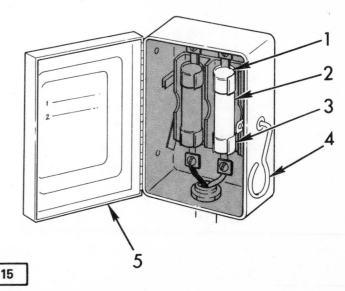

ELECTRICAL

Circuit Checkout — Fuses

1. Insert electrical plugs into outlets [1] one at a time. Place switches [2] to ON one at a time.

The appliance that was plugged in or the switch turned on when fuse [3] blows or button [4] trips, is defective.

The appliance should be repaired or a repair-man called.

If fuse [3] blows or button [4] trips only when all switches are turned on or all appliances are plugged in and turned on, one or more appliances will have to be moved from that fuse's circuit to another circuit to reduce the electrical load.

If fuse [3] does not blow or button [4] does not trip a second time, you have solved the problem.

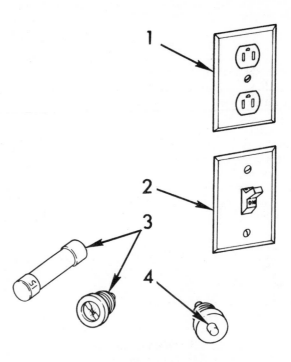

ELECTRICAL

Reset Circuit Breakers

1. Open cover [1] of circuit breaker box [3].

2. Check for circuit breaker [2] in middle or OFF position, or for pushbutton [4] which sticks out further than other pushbuttons.

Refer to your sketch or label inside circuit breaker door to determine switches and outlets controlled by this circuit breaker.

3. Place all wall switches to OFF. Remove electrical plugs from outlets controlled by circuit breaker.

4. Place circuit breaker [2] to RESET or full OFF position, then to ON position.

If circuit breaker [2] does not remain in ON position, wait one minute to repeat Step 4.

If circuit breaker remains in ON position, close circuit breaker box cover. Go to next page to check out circuit.

If circuit breaker [2] still does not remain in ON position, you should call an electrical repairman.

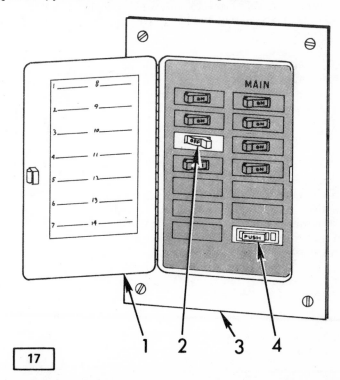

ELECTRICAL

Circuit Checkout — Circuit Breakers

1. Insert electrical plugs into outlets [1] one at
    a time. Place all switches [2] to ON one at
    a time.

The appliance that was plugged in or the switch
that was turned on when circuit breaker [3] or
pushbutton [4] "trips" or goes to OFF, is
defective.

The appliance should be repaired, or a repairman
called.

If circuit breaker [3] or pushbutton [4] "trips"
or goes to OFF only when all switches are turned
on or all appliances are plugged in and turned on,
one or more appliances will have to be moved
from that circuit breaker's circuit to reduce the
electrical load.

If circuit breaker [3] remains at ON position you
have solved the problem.

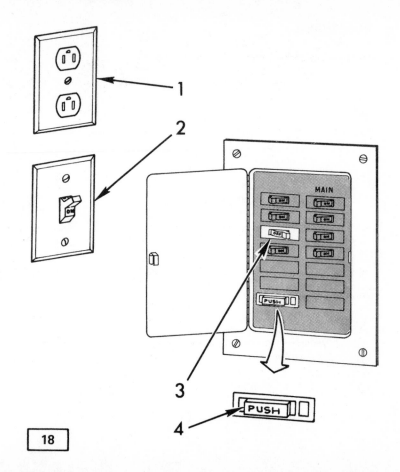

ELECTRICAL

Replace Wall Switches

WARNING

Be sure to turn off circuit breaker or remove fuse that controls power to wall switch being replaced. Page 12.

1. Remove screws [1]. Remove face plate [2].

2. Remove two mounting screws [3].

3. Pull switch [4] from box [5].

To help you remember where each wire connects, label and note position of each wire [6] before removing it.

4. Loosen screws [7]. Remove wires from screws. Remove switch.

To be sure of exact replacement, take old switch with you to hardware store.

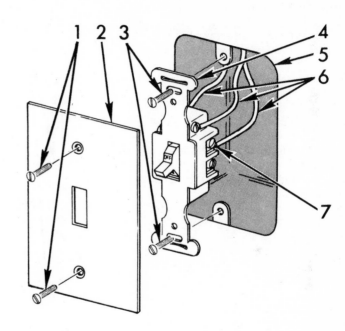

ELECTRICAL

Replace Wall Switches

5. Install wires [6] on screws [7] of new switch. Tighten screws. Remove labels.

6. Place switch [4] in box [5]. Install two mounting screws [3].

7. Install face plate [2]. Install screws [1].

8. Place circuit breaker to ON or install fuse.

9. Place switch to ON and OFF to check operation.

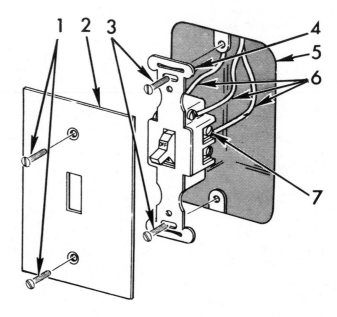

ELECTRICAL

Replace Wall Outlets

WARNING

Be sure to turn off circuit breaker or remove fuse that controls power to wall outlet being replaced. Page 12.

1.   Remove screw [1]. Remove face plate [2].

2.   Remove two mounting screws [3].

3.   Pull outlet [4] from box [5].

To help you remember where each wire connects, label and note position of each wire [6] before removing it.

4.   Loosen screws [7]. Remove wires [6] from screws. Remove outlet [4].

To be sure of exact replacement, take old outlet with you to hardware store.

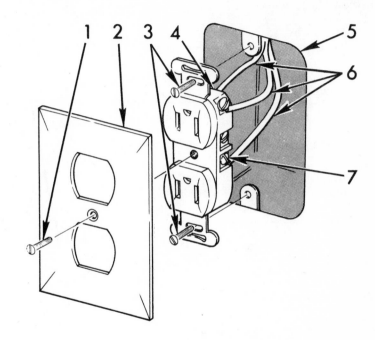

ELECTRICAL

Replace Wall Outlets

5. Install wires [5] on screws [6] of new outlet. Tighten screws. Remove labels.

6. Place outlet [4] in box [7]. Install two mounting screws [3].

7. Install face plate [2]. Install screw [1].

8. Place circuit breaker to ON or install fuse.

9. Insert electrical plug of appliance or lamp into outlet [4]. Check operation of appliance or lamp.

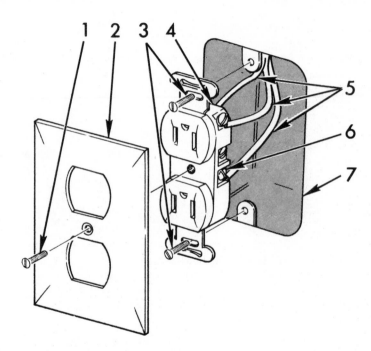

ELECTRICAL

Repair Appliance Cord Plug

To perform this section, you will need a common or Phillips screwdriver and knife or diagonal cutting pliers.

If repairing male two or three pronged plug [1], go to Page 25.

1. Remove plug casing [2] from contacts [7] and spring guard [3] by removing screws [8] and nuts [6].

2. Loosen two terminal screws [5]. Pull cord [4] through spring guard [3].

If repairing cord [4] only, go to next page.

If changing plug casing [2] only, go to next page, Step 5.

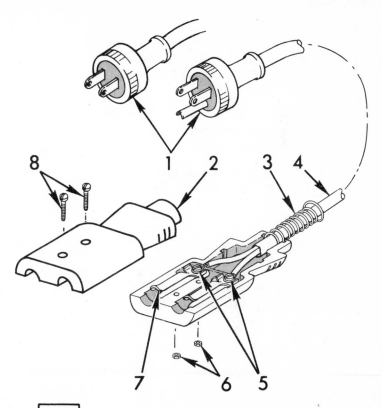

ELECTRICAL

Repair Appliance Cord Plug

3. Cut off damaged end of cord [2]. Using a knife or diagonal cutting pliers, carefully remove 2-1/2 inches of outside insulation [4].

4. Remove 3/4-inch of wire insulation [5] from each wire end [6].

5. Insert cord [2] through spring guard [1]. Bend each wire end [6] into hook shape.

6. Place wire ends [6] around terminal screws [3] in same direction as screws will be tightened. Tighten screws.

7. Place spring guard [1] into one half of new plug casing [7]. Install other half of new casing. Install screws [8] and nuts [9].

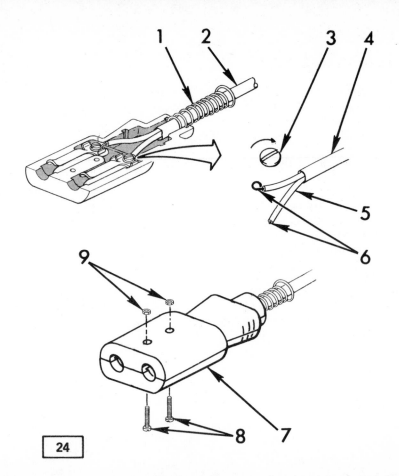

ELECTRICAL

Repair Appliance Cord Plug

8.   Remove insulator [1].

9.   Loosen screws [6]. Remove wires [5] from screws. Cut or untie knot [7].

10. Pull cord [9] through center hole in plug [8].

11. Cut off damaged end of cord [9]. Using a knife or diagonal cutting pliers, carefully remove 2-1/2 inches of outside insulation [2].

12. Remove 3/4-inch of wire insulation [3] from each wire end [4].

13. Insert cord [9] through center hole in plug [8].

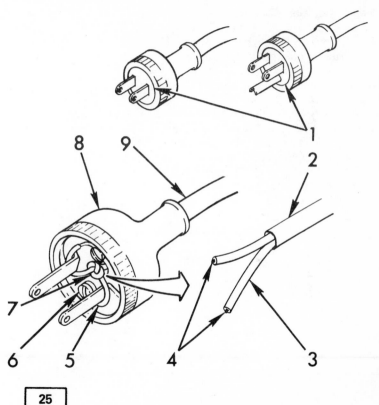

ELECTRICAL

Repair Appliance Cord Plug

14. Tie knot [3] in wires. Pull cord [1] from
    back of plug [2] until it stops.

If plug [2] has three prongs [7], green wire
must go on green screw.

15. Place wire ends [5] around terminal
    screws [4] in same direction as screws
    will be tightened. Tighten screws.

16. Install insulator [6].

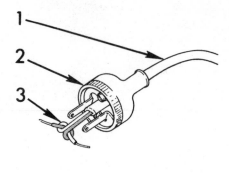

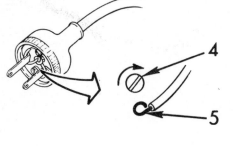

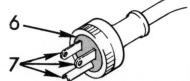

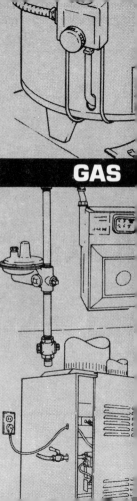

GAS

GAS

You should be familiar with your gas system and gas appliances.

If any problems arise with your gas system it is recommended that you immediately call the Gas Company.

CAUTION

To prevent fire or damage to your gas appliances such as a furnace or water heater, the area around the burner should be cleaned periodically.

To aid you in emergencies and finding leaks, draw the floor plan of your home in the space provided on next page. Locate and sketch the following items in the floor plan:

- Main gas shutoff valve [1] located close to your gas meter [3].

- Individual (gas appliance) shutoff valves [2] for furnace, water heater, range and oven, clothes dryer and gas fireplaces.

Generally, shutoff valves [2] will be found beside or behind these appliances.

If you have difficulty in locating these items, you may wish to ask the gas meter man to point them out to you on his next visit.

If floor plan space on opposite page is not large enough, draw floor plan on separate sheet of paper and attach to opposite page.

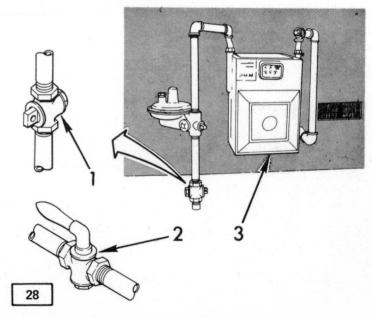

28

HOME FLOOR PLAN

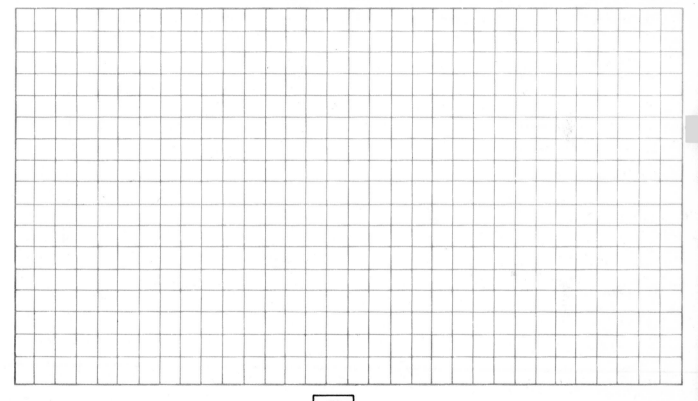

GAS

Leak Detection

For your safety, the gas companies have mixed a substance in with the gas used in your home, so that the gas has an odor.

This odor makes it easier to detect a leak. If a leak is detected, follow these important steps:

WARNING

DO NOT use a flame to locate leak.

DO NOT place light [2] or vent switch [1] to ON if odor is very strong. Switch could spark causing an explosion.

_____

If room is dark, use a flashlight. If odor is very strong, emergency steps on next page must be followed.

1. Open windows and doors if odor is slight. Locate leak by following odor.

If problem is simply a pilot light out, see section on lighting pilot lights. If not, turn off shutoff valve [3] behind or beside the appliance and call Gas Company.

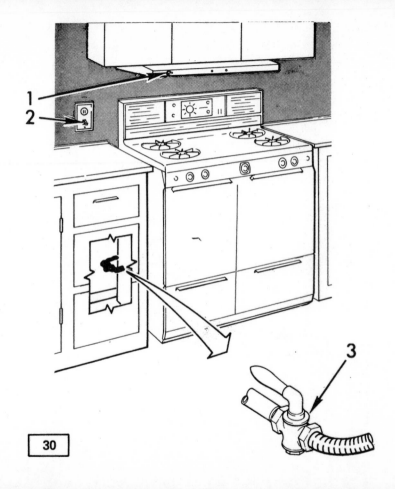

GAS

Emergency Action

If a gas leak is caused by a general emergency, such as a natural disaster, do the following:

1.   Turn off main gas shutoff valve [1] with wrench, if time and safety permit.

2.   Open all windows and doors.

3.   Vacate the house.

WARNING

Be sure everyone is out of house. Call Gas Company. Do not go back into house until it is free of all gas odors and no evidence of leakage remains.

DO NOT turn gas back on. Let Gas Company do it for you when they decide it is safe.

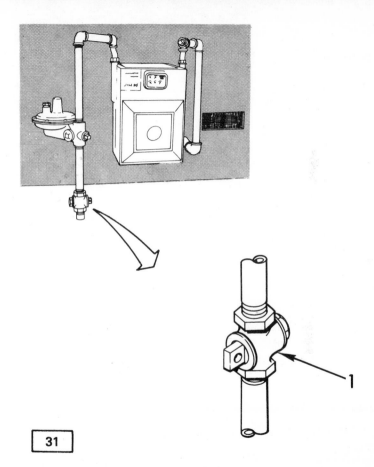

GAS

Furnace — Lighting the Pilot

To locate pilot light [4] start at shutoff valve [3] and follow gas pipe [2] into furnace.

You may have to remove a panel [1] to get to pilot light.

Generally, the manufacturer will have instructions written near pilot light [4]. Follow his instructions

If you cannot light pilot, call your local Gas Company.

> **If your gas furnace has a blower, it will have a filter near the blower. Check the filter periodically and clean or replace it per manufacturer's instructions.**

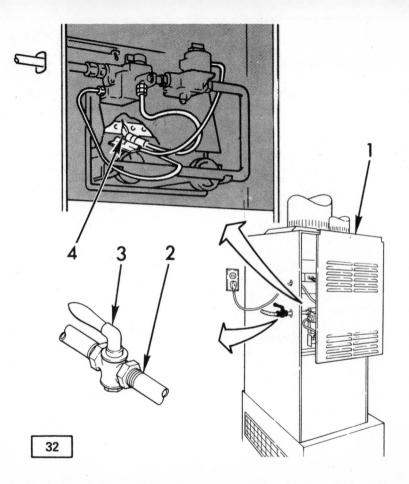

GAS

Gas Range — Lighting the Top Burner Pilots

Your gas range has several pilot lights. Pilot light [1] ignites burners [2] when gas is turned on.

The pilot light shown in the illustration is typical. Even if yours does not look like the one shown, it works the same way.

WARNING

Pilot lights must be kept lit at all times.

When pilot light is out, a small amount of gas flows out of pilot light nozzle.

1. Remove grids [3]. Remove cover [4].

2. Light pilot [1] with match.

3. Install cover [4]. Install grid [3].

4. Turn on gas valves [5]. Check that burners [2] ignite.

WARNING

If burners [2] do not ignite, turn them off and call Gas Company.

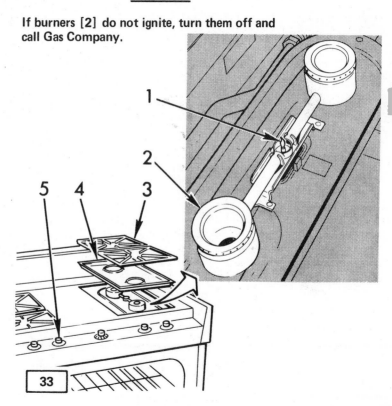

33

GAS

Gas Range — Lighting the Oven Pilot

Appearance and location of oven pilot light [4] will differ with the various makes of gas ranges.

Some gas oven pilot lights can be lit without removing insides of oven.

1. Open broiler [2].

2. Check broiler to see if pilot light [4] is accessible.

3. Light pilot [4] with match if accessible.

If you cannot reach pilot light, go to next page.

4. Turn on oven valve [1]. Check that oven burner [3] ignites.

<u>WARNING</u>

If pilot light will not stay lit, turn valve [1] off and call Gas Company.

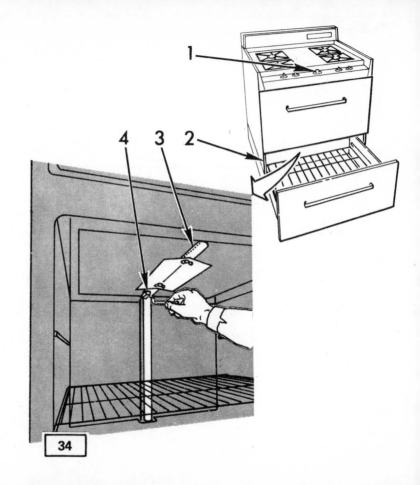

34

GAS

Gas Range — Lighting the Oven Pilot

Appearance and location of oven pilot [4] will differ with the various makes of gas ranges.

5. Remove racks [5]. Remove tray [2].

6. Light pilot [4] with match.

7. Install tray [2]. Install racks [5].

8. Turn on oven valve [1]. Check that oven burner [3] ignites.

WARNING

If pilot light will not stay lit, turn valve [1] off and call Gas Company.

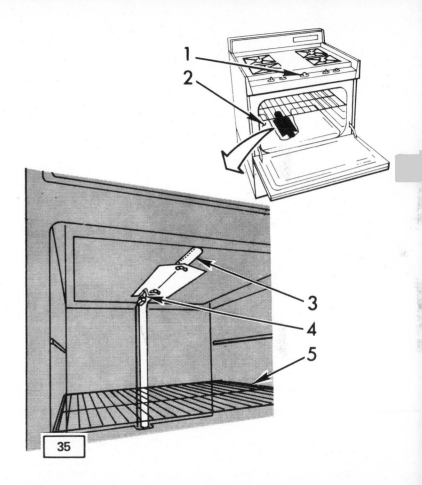

35

GAS

Water Heater — Lighting the Pilot

1. Remove panel [3].

2. Remove plate [2] if installed on your
   water heater.

Generally, the manufacturer will have instructions
near pilot [1]. Follow his instructions.

3. Light pilot [1] with match.

WARNING

If pilot light does not ignite, call Gas Company.

4. Install plate [2]. Install panel [3].

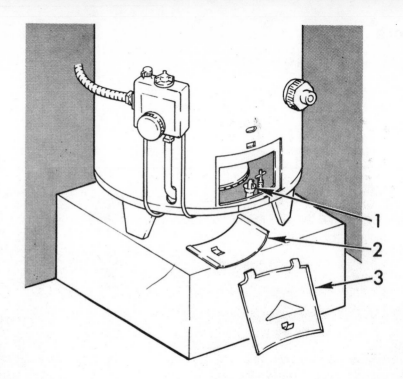

PLUMBING

PLUMBING

Being familiar with the location of water shutoff valves in your home is useful whenever an emergency arises or when making minor plumbing repairs. The information in this section will help you locate these important items.

In areas of the country where freezing winter temperatures are common, water meters are generally located in basements or other protected locations in houses. The meter shutoff valve and house main shutoff valve are generally located near the water meter.

In areas of the country where winters are mild and water lines need not be protected from freezing, water meters are generally located under front sidewalks or near front street curbs. They are generally covered by small concrete covers. The house main shutoff valve is generally located outside the house near a hose faucet.

Individual water shutoff valves are generally located very near the plumbing fixture for which they are provided.

If you cannot locate your water meter [2] or main shutoff valve [1] in or around your home, your water meter man will be glad to show you during his next visit.

Draw the floor plan of your home in the space provided on next page. Locate the following items and sketch them into your floor plan:

- Water meter [2] and meter shutoff valve [1]
- House main shutoff valve [3]
- Individual water shutoff valves [4] (for sinks, toilets, washing machine, etc.)

If an overflow or sudden flooding is the problem, turn off house main valve [3] or meter shutoff valve [1], then locate the problem.

If floor plan space on next page is not large enough, draw floor plan on separate sheet of paper and attach to page.

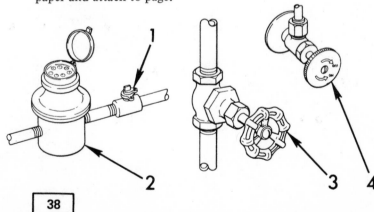

HOME FLOOR PLAN

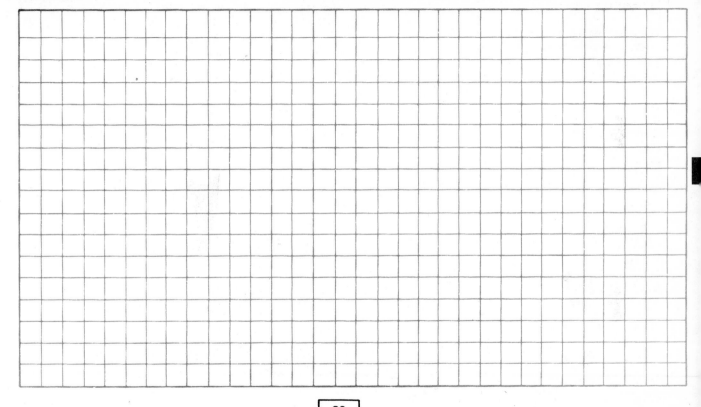

PLUMBING

Many plumbing problems must be handled by an expert. However, many ordinary plumbing repairs around the home are not difficult to perform yourself.

The tools required for most repairs are common and not expensive.

This section provides basic repairs for the most common causes of plumbing problems connected with drains, faucets and toilets.

If you have a problem and a plumber is called, be sure to watch what he does. **NEXT TIME** you may be able to do it yourself, thereby saving money.

Whenever replacing any plumbing part, such as a washer or toilet float ball, be sure to take the old part with you to the store to insure exact replacement of that part.

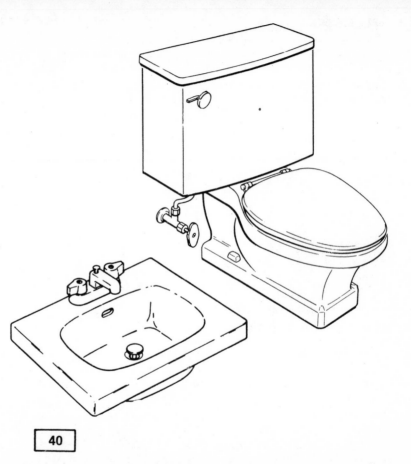

PLUMBING

Water Leak Test

If a hidden water leak is suspected in your home, the following simple test should be followed:

1. Turn off all faucets and water outlets.

The leak test is made by observing pointer on one-cubic-foot scale [1] or ten-gallon scale [2] of your water meter. Observe pointer periodically for a period of at least 15 minutes.

2. While observing water meter scales [1 or 2], check for any movement of pointer.

If pointer on scale moves at all, your home has a water leak. Call a plumber if you cannot locate and repair the leak yourself.

If pointer on scale moves rapidly, indicating a large water leak, turn off the main shutoff valve until repairs are made.

Water spots on ceilings, walls, or floors indicate water leakage. Check for evidence of this type regularly.

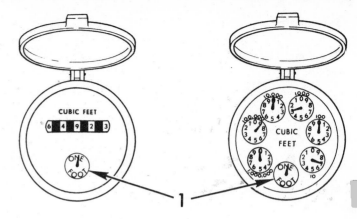

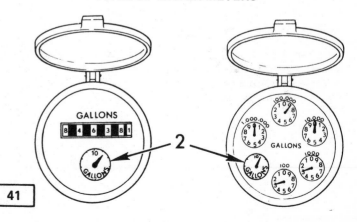

TYPES OF WATER METERS

41

PLUMBING

Drains

If drain [3] is clogged, you must determine if stoppage is localized to one drain [3] or if main drain [4] is clogged.

<u>CAUTION</u>

Do not flush toilets to determine location of stoppage. Flushing toilet releases a large amount of water and may cause an overflow.

1. Turn on water in sink [1] in another part of house for about 3 minutes or until sink [1] fills.

2. Check that drain [2] is not clogged.

If drain [2] is also clogged, the main drain [4] is clogged. Call a plumber to correct this problem.

If sink [1] drains freely the problem is in drain [3]. To unclog sink, shower and bathtub drains, go to next page.

To unclog toilet drains, go to Page 73.

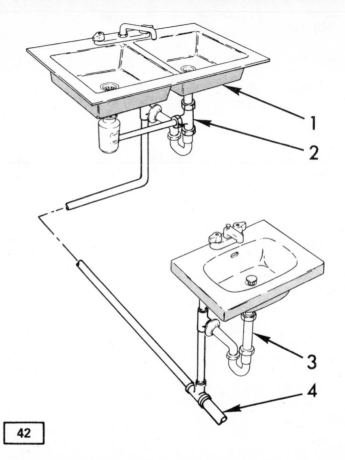

42

PLUMBING

Drains

This section shows how to clear drain clog by the following methods:

- Cleaning strainer [3] or stopper [1]

- Using a plunger [4]

- Cleaning out trap [2]

- Clearing clog with chemicals

- Using a drain auger [5]

If you do have to call a plumber and you have recently used a chemical drain cleaner, be sure to tell him.

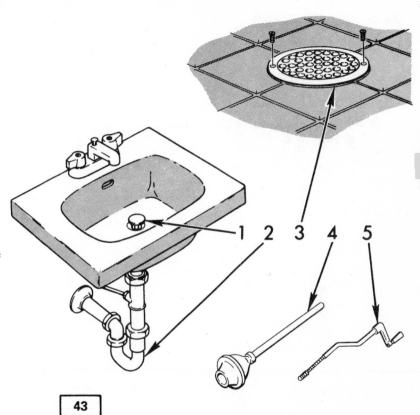

PLUMBING

Drains — Cleaning Strainer

1. Carefully remove screws [2] from strainer [1].

2. Remove strainer [1] by lifting.

3. Clean strainer [1]. Clean drain opening as far as you can reach.

4. Install strainer [1]. Install screws [2].

If cleaning strainer [1] does not clear the drain, go to Page 46.

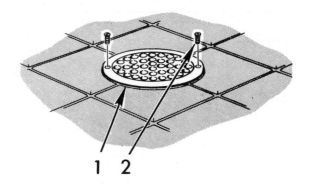

1 2

PLUMBING

Drains — Cleaning Stopper

1. Remove stopper [1] by turning
    counterclockwise and lifting.

If stopper [1] cannot be removed this way,
go to Step 4.

2. Clean stopper [1]. Clean drain opening as
    far as you can reach.

3. Install stopper [1] by turning clockwise.

If cleaning the stopper [1] does not clear the
drain, go to the next page.

4. Place container under pipe [6].

5. Loosen screw [2]. Remove nut [4] from
    pipe [6]. Remove rod [3] from pipe [6].

6. Remove stopper [7] by lifting. Clean
    stopper. Clean drain opening as far as you
    can reach.

7. Install stopper [7]. Insert rod [3] into
    hole [5]. Install nut [4]. Tighten screw [2].

8. Remove container. Turn on faucet.

If cleaning stopper [7] does not clear drain, go to
next page.

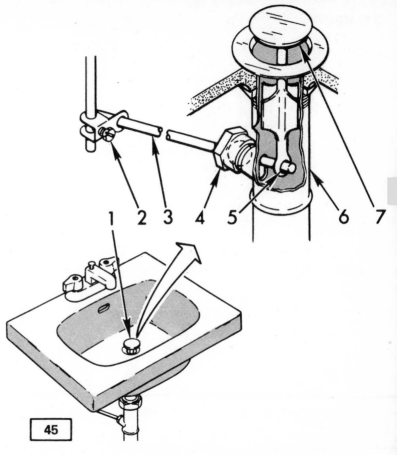

45

PLUMBING

Drains — Using a Plunger

To perform this section, you will need a plunger [3 or 4].

Either type [3] or [4] may be used. However, the molded type [3] is generally more efficient.

1. Remove stopper [2] or strainer [1]. Page 45 or 44.

2. Apply a thick coating of petroleum jelly around base [5] of plunger [3 or 4].

3. Turn on water until there is approximately 2-inches of water in sink, tub or shower.

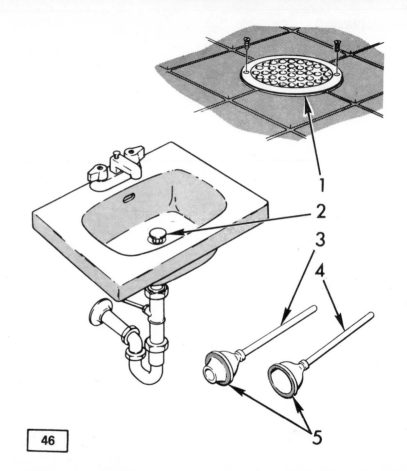

PLUMBING

Drains — Using a Plunger

Plunger [5] will work better if damp cloth is placed in overflow opening [2]. This increases the suction of plunger.

4. Place plunger [5] over drain [4].

5. Move plunger up and down five to ten times.

Be patient, it may take time to completely clear drain. Repeat Steps 4 and 5 several times.

6. Turn on water.

If drain is still not clear, go to next page.

If drain is clear, continue on.

7. Install stopper [3] or strainer [1].
    Page 45 or 44.

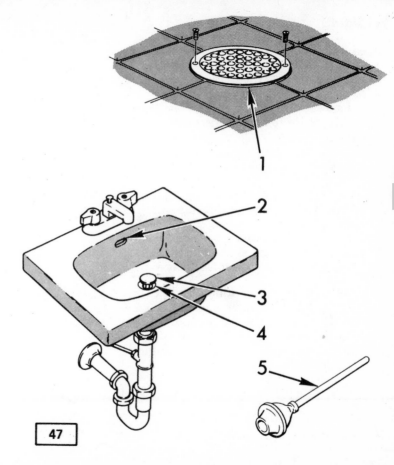

PLUMBING

Drains — Cleaning Out the Trap

WARNING

If you have already used a chemical drain cleaner, wear rubber gloves to avoid contact with chemical drain cleaner.

1. Place container directly under trap [1].

If your trap [1] does not have a plug [2], go to next page. If plug is present, continue on.

2. Using wrench or channellock pliers, remove plug [2] by turning as illustrated [4]. Wait until all waste water has drained.

3. Cut off hook of wire clothes hanger [3]. Bend one end of hanger into small hook.

4. Push hook into trap [1] and pull it out until clog has been cleared. Clean out trap opening with small brush or rag.

5. Install plug [2] by turning as illustrated [4]. Turn on water.

If drain is still not clear, go to Page 50.

48

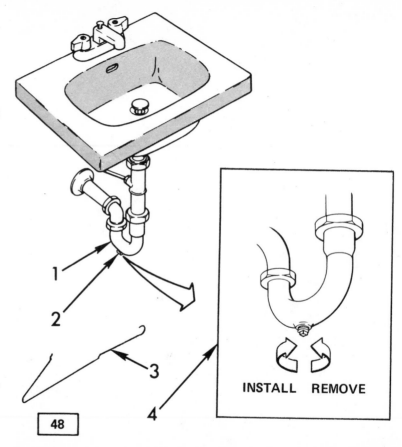

INSTALL   REMOVE

PLUMBING

Drains — Cleaning Out the Trap

CAUTION

Before using a wrench, protect the finish of all chrome (shiny) pipes and fixtures by wrapping them with two layers of adhesive tape.

6. Loosen two slip nuts [1] by turning as illustrated with wrench or channellock pliers.

7. Remove trap [2].

8. Clean trap [2] with piece of wire and small brush or rag.

9. Check that two washers [3] are not damaged.

If washers [3] are damaged, take washers to your local hardware store for replacement.

10. While holding trap [2] firmly in position, tighten the two slip nuts [1] by turning as illustrated.

11. Turn on water

12. Remove tape from fixtures.

If drain is still not clear, continue to next page.

49

PLUMBING

Drains — Clearing with Chemicals

To perform this section, you will need a funnel
and a commercial drain cleaner. Keep funnel
and use it for this purpose only.

Be sure to follow the warnings and directions on
label of container [2].

1. Remove stopper [4] or strainer [3].
    Page 45 or 44.

2. Place funnel [1] in drain opening [5].

3. Pour measured amount of cleaner into
    drain [5]. Remove and rinse funnel [1].

Allow cleaner to work as stated on label before
turning water on.

4. Turn on water.

If drain is still not clear, continue to next page.

If drain is clear, continue on.

5. Install stopper [4] or strainer [3].
    Page 45 or 44.

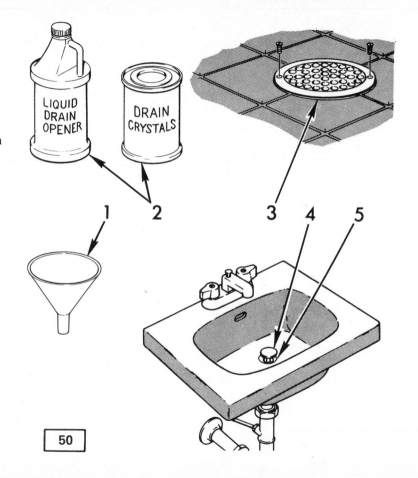

PLUMBING

Drains — Using a Drain Auger

1. Remove stopper [2] or strainer [3].
   Page 45 or 44.

CAUTION

Do not force drain auger [4] into drain.

2. Push auger [4] into drain [5] until it stops.

Always turn handle [1] in one direction only.

3. While turning handle [1] push auger further
   into drain [5] until auger moves freely in
   pipe [6].

Free movement of auger [4] in the pipe [6]
means you have removed the clog.

4. Remove auger [4]. Install stopper [2] or
   strainer [3]. Page 45 or 44.

If drain [5] is still not clear, go to next page.

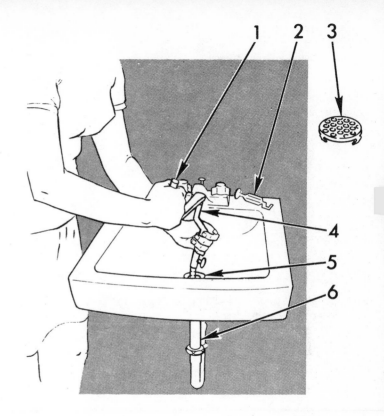

PLUMBING

Drains — Using a Drain Auger

WARNING

Wear rubber gloves to avoid contact with chemical drain cleaner.

5. Remove plug [3] or trap [2]. Page 48.

6. Push drain auger [4] into pipe [1] until it stops.

Always turn handle [5] in one direction only.

7. While turning handle [5] push auger further into pipe [1] until auger moves freely in pipe.

Free movement of auger [4] in pipe [1] means you have removed the clog.

8. Install plug [3] or trap [2]. Page 48.

9. Pour boiling water into sink. Check that drain is working. Turn on water.

Your drain should be clear. However, if it is not, a plumber should be called. Be sure to tell him you have recently used a drain cleaner.

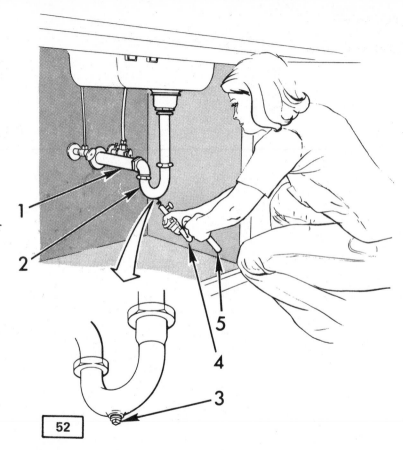

52

PLUMBING

Garbage Disposer

<u>**WARNING**</u>

Be sure garbage disposer switch [3] remains OFF while working on garbage disposer.

1. Place garbage disposer switch [3] to OFF.

2. Remove all foreign objects and debris from garbage disposer [2].

Reset button [1] may be on side or on bottom of garbage disposer [2].

3. Depress, and release reset button [1].

4. Turn water on. Allow water to drain into disposer [2].

5. Place switch [3] to ON. Go to next page.

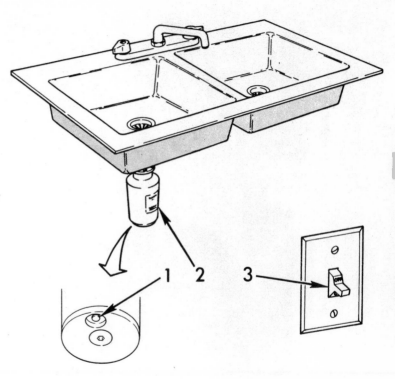

PLUMBING

Garbage Disposer

6. If disposer still does not work, place switch [3] to OFF. Turn water off.

7. Check bottom of disposer for Hex key slot [1]. Insert Hex key [2] in slot.

Turning Hex key clockwise or counterclockwise will verify disposer shaft is not stuck.

8. Turn key [2] clockwise or counterclockwise.

If key will not turn, call a plumber. If key will turn, continue on.

9. Remove key [2].

10. Turn water on. Place switch [3] to ON.

If disposer still does not work, turn water off and call a plumber.

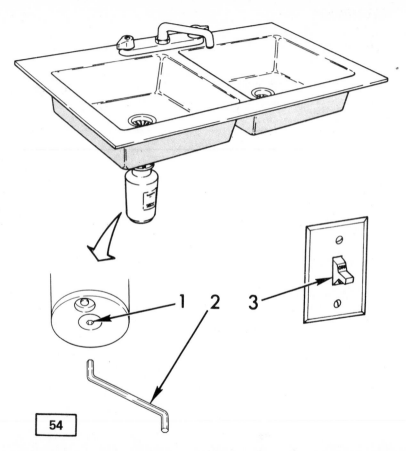

54

PLUMBING

Faucets

Some faucets may not look exactly the same as faucets [2] shown at right; however, all faucets come apart easily and in a similar manner.

Most single lever faucets [1] cannot be repaired, except by a plumber.

Leaks should be repaired as soon as they are noticed. Leaking faucets can cause stains, wasted water, and damage to fixtures.

Faucet repairs are usually simple and, with the proper tools, can be done quickly and inexpensively.

Take old parts removed from faucets to hardware store with you to be sure of exact replacement.

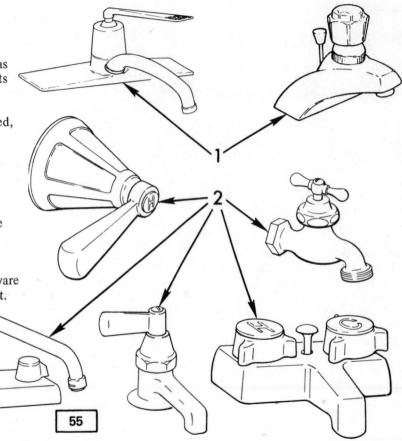

PLUMBING

Faucets

All faucets [9] are basically the same.

They consist of the following parts:

- Handle screw [1]
- Handle [2]
- Packing nut [3]
- Packing material [4]
- Washer [5]
- Stem [6]
- Washers [7]
- Seat [8]

Although there may be some variation due to differences in manufacture, the components listed generally apply to all brands of faucets.

Worn washers [5,7] or packing material [4] are usually the cause of faucet leaks.

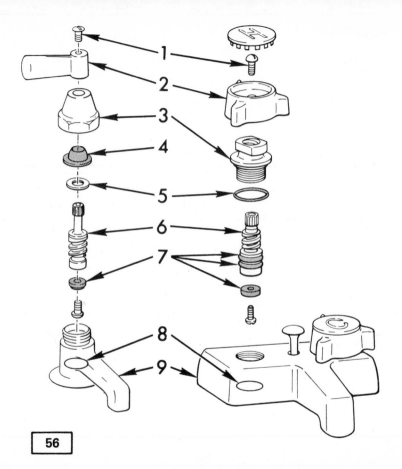

PLUMBING

Faucets

The illustrations on this page show the most common leaks that could occur.

If faucet is leaking from the spout [3,5,6], go to Page 65.

If faucet is leaking from the stem [1,4,8,9], go to Page 61.

Base leaks from a single faucet [10], hose connection faucet [11] or shower faucet handle [12] are difficult to repair. A plumber should be called for this repair.

If your faucet is leaking from the base [2], go to Page 58.

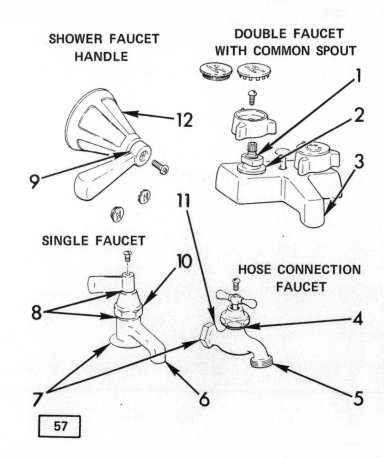

SHOWER FAUCET HANDLE

DOUBLE FAUCET WITH COMMON SPOUT

SINGLE FAUCET

HOSE CONNECTION FAUCET

57

PLUMBING

Faucets — Base Leak

If faucets do not have individual shutoff valves [4], main valve must be closed. Page 38.

1. Turn off water shutoff valve [4] to faucet.

2. Turn on faucet until all water has drained.

Some handle screws [2] may be under screw-in or snap-in caps [1].

3. Remove cap [1] if installed. Remove screw [2].

You may have to tap handle [3] or move it back and forth to remove it.

4. Remove handle [3] by pulling off.

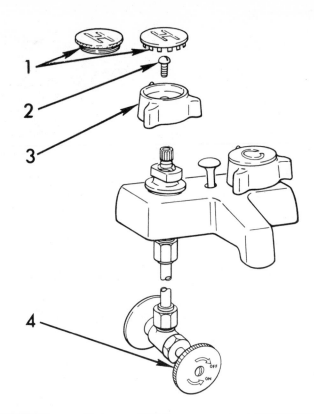

PLUMBING

Faucets — Base Leak

<u>CAUTION</u>

Before using a wrench, protect the finish of all chrome (shiny) pipes and fixtures by wrapping them with two layers of adhesive tape.

5.   Using adjustable wrench or channellock pliers, remove packing nut [1] by turning counterclockwise.

6.   Insert screwdriver between packing nut [1] and washer [2], to remove washer from packing nut.

Be sure replacement washer is same size and type.

7.   Carefully place new washer [2] on packing nut [1], until washer fits snugly against nut.

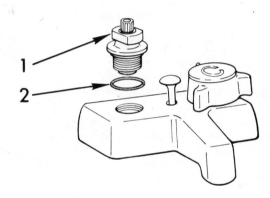

PLUMBING

Faucets — Base Leak

8. Install packing nut [4]. Using adjustable wrench or channellock pliers, tighten packing nut by turning clockwise.

9. Install handle [3].

10. Install screw [2]. Tighten screw. Install cap [1] if removed.

11. Turn handle [3] until faucet is completely shut off.

12. Turn on water shutoff valve [5] or main shutoff valve. Page 38.

13. Turn on faucet. Check for leaks.

If faucet still leaks faucet stem could be leaking, go to next page.

If your faucet handle [3] does not align with opposite handle, you may want to align them. Go to Page 68 to align handles.

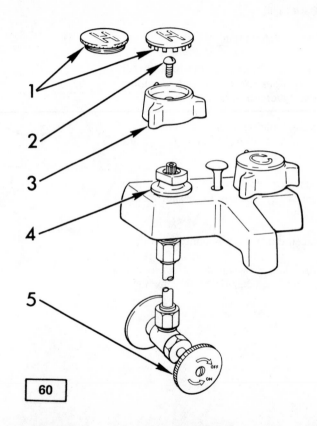

PLUMBING

Faucets — Stem Leak

If faucets do not have individual shutoff valves [5], main valve must be closed. Page 38.

1. Turn off water shutoff valve [5] to faucet.

2. Turn on faucet until all water has drained.

Some handle screws [2,6] may be under screw-in or snap-in caps [1,4].

3. Remove cap [1,4], if installed. Remove screw [2,6].

You may have to tap handle [3,7] or move it back and forth to remove it.

4. Remove handle [3,7] by pulling off.

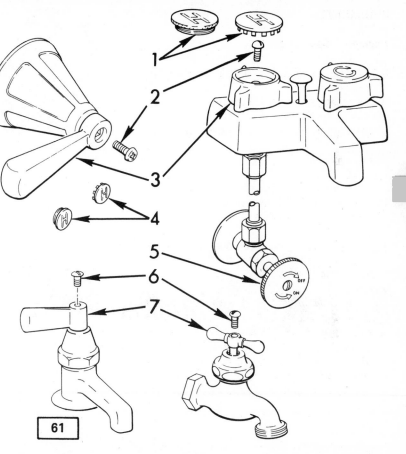

61

PLUMBING

Faucet — Stem Leak

CAUTION

Before using a wrench, protect the finish of all chrome (shiny) pipes and fixtures by wrapping them with two layers of adhesive tape.

If not working on shower faucet, go to Step 6.

5. Using channellock pliers, remove cover [2] of shower faucet by turning counterclockwise.

6. Using adjustable wrench or channellock pliers, remove packing nut [4] by turning counterclockwise.

7. Hold packing nut [4] with wrench. Place handle [1] over stem [3]. Turn handle [1]. Remove stem [3] from packing nut [4].

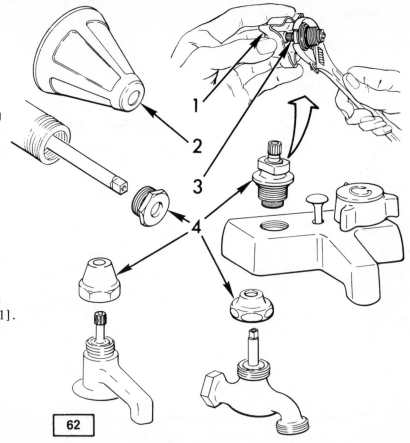

62

PLUMBING

Faucets — Stem Leak

8.   Remove washer [3] or packing [6] from stem [2] or packing nut [5].

9.   Install new packing [6] inside packing nut [5] or new washer [3] on stem [2].

Be sure packing or washers fit snugly.

10. Insert stem [2] through packing nut [1]. Tighten fingertight.

11. Install packing nut [5,1]. Using adjustable wrench or channellock pliers, tighten packing nut by turning clockwise.

If not working on shower faucet, go to Step 15.

12. Install chrome cover [4] on shower faucet by turning clockwise.

13. Using channellock pliers tighten chrome cover [4].

14. Remove adhesive tape from chrome fittings.

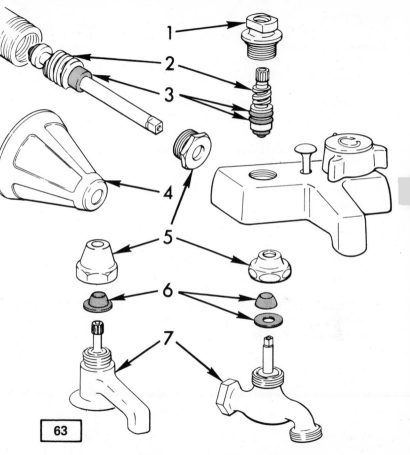

PLUMBING

Faucets — Stem Leak

15. Install handle [3,7].

16. Install screw [2,6]. Tighten screw [2,6].
    Install cap [1,4], if removed.

17. Turn handle [3,7] until faucet is completely
    shut off.

18. Turn on water shutoff valve [5] or main
    shutoff valve. Page 38.

19. Turn on faucet. Check for leaks.

If faucet still leaks, faucet could have a spout
leak, go to next page.

If your faucet handle [3,7] does not align with
opposite handle you may want to align them.
Go to Page 68 to align handles.

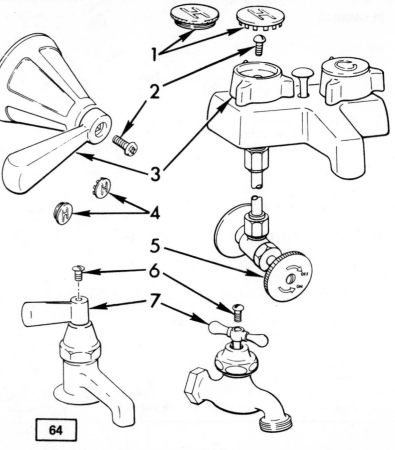

64

PLUMBING

Faucets — Spout Leak

If faucet is a shower faucet or double faucet
with common spout and does not have
individual shutoff valves, you should repair
both the hot and the cold faucets.

If faucet does not have individual shutoff
valve [5], main valve must be closed.
See Page 38.

1. Turn off one water shutoff valve [5]
    located directly under hot or cold
    faucet. Check that dripping has
    stopped.

If dripping has stopped, faucet above shutoff valve [5] is leaking.

If dripping has not stopped, the opposite
faucet is leaking.

2. Turn off shutoff valve [5] to leaking
    faucet. Turn on faucet until all water
    has drained.

Some handle screws [2,6] may be under screw-in
or snap-in caps [1,4].

3. Remove cap [1,4] if installed. Remove
    screw [2,6].

You may have to tap handle or move it back
and forth to remove it.

4. Remove handle [3,7] by pulling off.

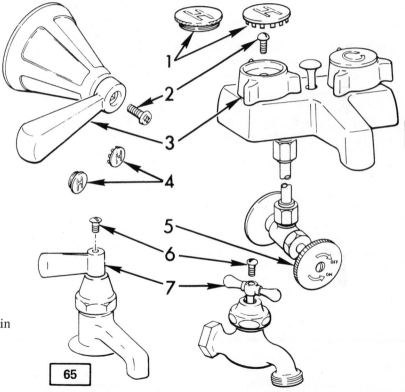

65

PLUMBING

Faucets — Spout Leak

<u>CAUTION</u>

Before using a wrench, protect the finish of all chrome (shiny) pipes and fixtures by wrapping them with two layers of adhesive tape.

If not working on shower faucet, go to Step 6.

5. Using channellock pliers remove cover [4] by turning counterclockwise.

6. Using adjustable wrench or channellock pliers, remove packing nut [1,5] by turning counterclockwise.

7. Remove brass screw [3,7].

If brass screw [3,7] is worn it should be replaced with one of same size.

8. Remove washer [2,6].

Be sure new washer is same size and type as old washer.

9. Install new washer [2,6]. Install brass screw [3,7]. Tighten screw [3,7].

10. Install packing nut [1,5]. Using adjustable wrench or channellock pliers, tighten packing nut by turning clockwise.

If not working on shower faucet, go to Step 13.

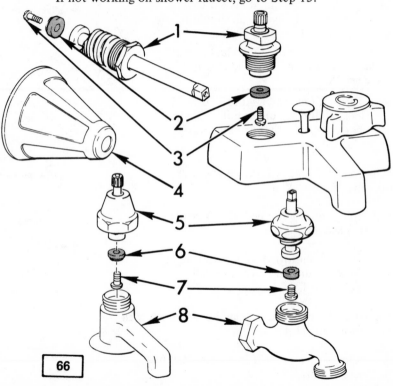

PLUMBING

Faucets — Spout Leak

11. Install cover [1] on shower faucet by turning clockwise. Using channellock pliers, tighten cover [1].

12. Remove adhesive tape from chrome fittings.

13. Install handle [4,8].

14. Install screw [3,7]. Tighten screw. Install cap [2,5], if removed.

15. Turn handle [4,8] until faucet is completely shut off.

16. Turn on water shutoff valve [6] or main shutoff valve. Page 38.

17. Turn on faucet. Check for leaks.

If your faucet handle [4,8] does not align with opposite handle, you may want to align them. Go to Page 68 to align handles.

If spout still leaks, call a plumber.

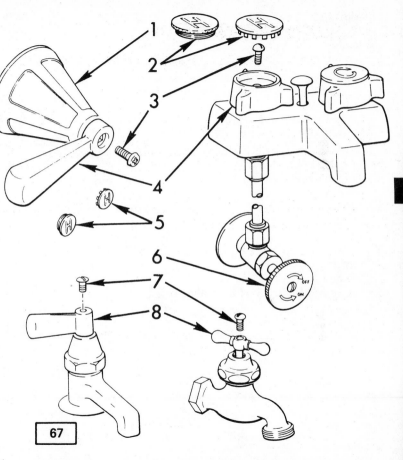

67

PLUMBING

Faucets — Align Handles

If your faucet handles [3,6] are not aligned with each other, you may want to align them.

1. Turn off water by turning faucet handles [3,6] to full off position.

Some handle screws [2,5] may be under screw-in or snap-caps [1,4].

2. Remove cap [1,4], if installed. Remove screw [2,5].

You may have to tap handle or move it back and forth to remove it.

3. Remove handle [3,6] by pulling off.

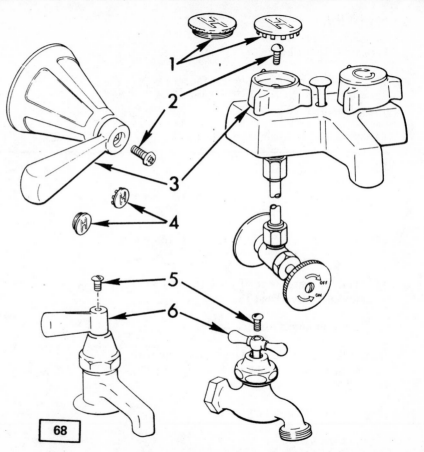

68

PLUMBING

Faucets — Align Handles

4. Place handle [3,6] in same position as opposite handle or in a position that allow handles freedom of movement for full flow of water.

5. Turn on hot and cold water faucet handles [3,6]. Turn handles to off position.

6. Check that alignment does not change. If position of handles changes, repeat Steps 4 and 5.

7. Install screw [2,5]. Tighten screw. Install cap [1,4], if removed.

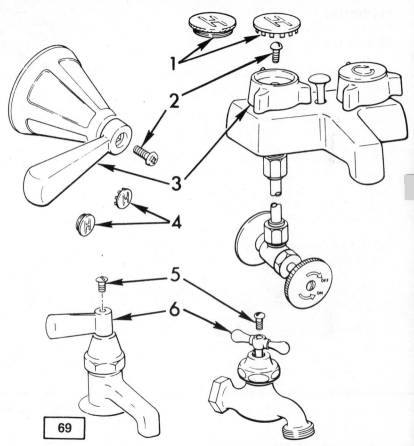

69

PLUMBING

Clean Aerator

1. Place a layer of adhesive tape around aerator [3] to protect finish.

2. Remove aerator [3] by turning clockwise.

3. Check that washer [1] is not worn. If washer [1] is worn, replace it with new one of same size and thickness.

4. Clean aerator [3] by holding upside down under running water.

5. Check for debris in filter [2]. If debris is present, clean it using a toothpick or pin.

6. Install aerator [3]. Tighten aerator by turning counterclockwise.

7. Remove adhesive tape from aerator.

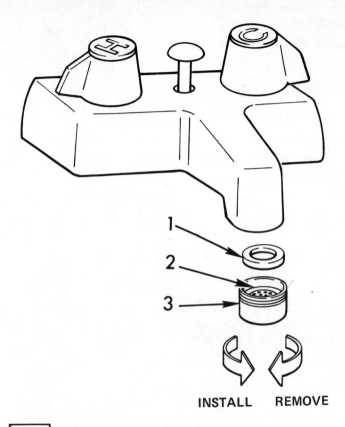

INSTALL   REMOVE

PLUMBING

Toilets

Most flush tank mechanisms are similar to the one at the right.

Some parts may look different, from those shown, but their function and methods of repair are generally the same.

The four most common problems covered in this section are:

- Clogged toilet (overflow)

- Running toilet (water running continuously into tank)

- Slow or no flush (handle must be held until flush is complete)

- Water leaking from base of tank

Before trying to repair the toilet, you should be familiar with the functions of toilet parts, as explained on the next page.

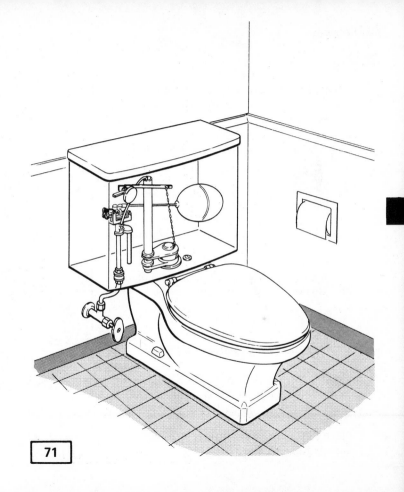

PLUMBING

Toilets

The mechanism within the tank is designed to produce enough water to completely flush the toilet bowl as explained in the following steps:

1. Depressing handle [3] causes flush ball [7] to rise.

2. Water in tank [5] then flows through flush ball opening into bowl [8].

3. Float ball [6] drops with level of water in tank [5].

4. Flush ball [7] sinks slowly back into place, shutting off the flow of water to the bowl.

5. As float ball arm [4] drops, it lifts inlet valve [2] in ballcock assembly [1] which controls the flow of water into the tank.

6. Fresh water flows through the ballcock assembly [1] into tank [5]. This causes float ball [6] to rise with level of water. As the float ball rises it depresses inlet valve [2] and shuts off water flow when tank is full.

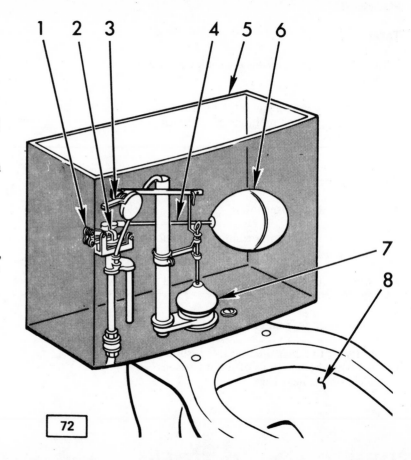

72

PLUMBING

Clogged Toilet

A clogged toilet is generally caused by an object caught in trap [4].

To perform the following steps you will need a plunger [1].

1. Pour water into bowl [2] until water level is just below rim [3].

2. Place suction cup [5] over toilet opening [6]. Move plunger [1] up and down until water drains from toilet.

If toilet drain is not clear, go to next page.

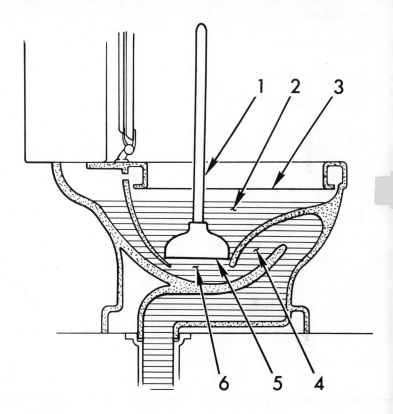

PLUMBING

Clogged Toilet

To perform steps on this page you will need a toilet auger [2]. If toilet auger is not available, any type auger will do.

If using any auger other than a toilet auger [2] be careful not to scratch bowl [3].

3. Push end of auger [2] into opening as far as it will go.

Always turn auger handle [1] in same direction.

4. While turning handle [1], push auger [2] into trap [4].

If this method does not clear toilet, clog is in main drain pipe, and a plumber should be called.

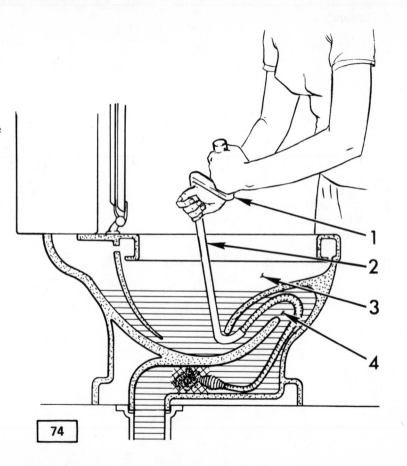

74

PLUMBING

Running Toilet

Follow the steps on this page to determine where the problem is:

1. Remove top [1] of tank [2]. Carefully place top where it will not be damaged.

2. Check water level in tank [2].

If water level is more than 1-inch below top of overflow tube [3], go to next page.

If water level is running into top of overflow tube [3], go to Page 80.

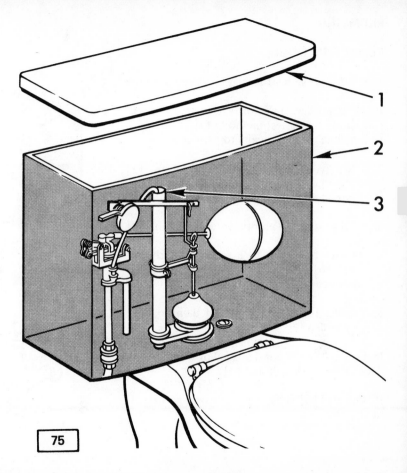

PLUMBING

Toilets — Flush Ball

1.   Turn off shutoff valve [8], if you have one.

If you don't have a shutoff valve [8], the next
step shows the easiest method of shutting off
water while making repairs to your toilet.

2.   Bend coat hanger [2] over top of tank [3].
Place hook [4] around float ball arm [1].
Bend hook to keep arm at highest position.

3.   Flush toilet to empty water from tank [3].

4.   Check that wire [5] is screwed tightly into
ball [6]. If it will not stay tight, go to
next page.

5.   Check flush ball [6] for any damage
or wear.

If flush ball [6] is not damaged or worn, go to
Page 78 to repair ball seat [7].

If flush ball [6] is damaged or worn, go to
next page.

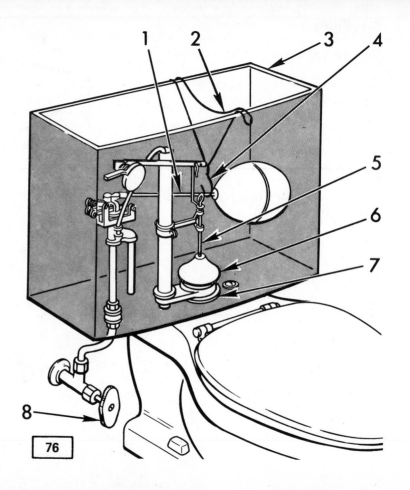

76

PLUMBING

Toilets — Flush Ball

Take old flush ball to hardware store to insure exact replacement. Perform following steps to replace flush ball.

6. While holding lift wire [2] up, remove flush ball [3] by turning clockwise.

7. Install new flush ball [3] on lift wire by turning counterclockwise.

8. Depress and release handle [1] several times. Check that flush ball [3] sits evenly on ball seat [4].

If flush ball [3] does not sit evenly on seat [4], go to Page 79 to align flush ball guide [5].

If flush ball [3] sits evenly on seat [4], go to next page.

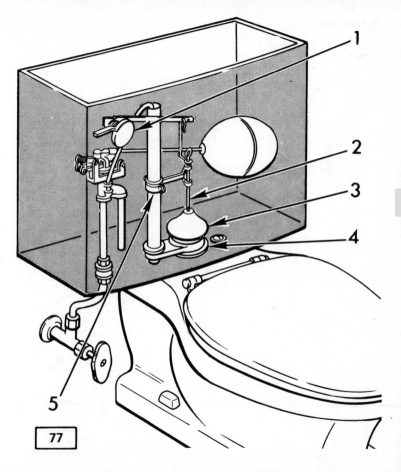

PLUMBING

Toilets — Flush Ball

In next step, emery cloth or steel wool may be used to clean ball seat [4].

9. Raise flush ball [3]. Clean top rim and inner surface of ball seat [4] until smooth.

10. Turn on shutoff valve [5] or remove coat hanger.

11. Check that toilet is not running and water level is approximately 1-inch from top of overflow tube [7].

If toilet is still running and water level is not 1-inch below top of overflow tube, go to next page.

12. Carefully place top [1] on tank.

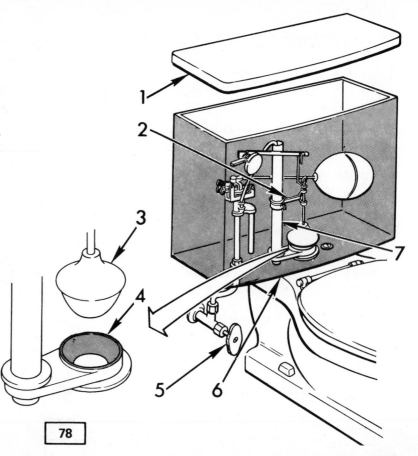

PLUMBING

Toilets — Flush Ball Guide

If flush ball [8] in your toilet is supported by a chain [9], simply adjust the length of the chain until the flush ball sits evenly on ball seat [7]. Go to Step 16.

If flush ball [8] is supported by a lift wire [3] and guide [6], perform the following steps to align the flush ball with the ball seat [7]:

13. Turn off shutoff valve [10] or install coat hanger. Page 76.

14. Loosen screw [5] in guide [6].

15. Move guide [6] left and right or up and down until the flush ball [8] sits evenly on ball seat [7]. Tighten screw [5].

16. Turn on shutoff valve [10] or remove coat hanger.

17. Flush toilet. Check that toilet now flushes correctly.

18. Carefully place top [1] on tank [4].

If toilet still does not flush correctly, a plumber should be called.

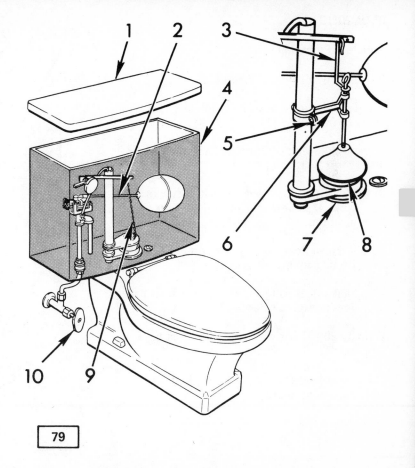

79

PLUMBING

Toilets — Float Ball

1. Gently lift float ball arm [2].

If water does not shut off, go to Page 82 for repair of inlet valve [1].

If water does shut off, problem is in float ball arm [2] or float ball [3].

2. Check that float is not touching side of tank. If float is touching side of tank, bend rod.

3. Remove float ball [3] from arm [2] by turning counterclockwise.

4. Shake float ball [3]. Check that float ball does not have water inside.

If float ball [3] has water inside, it must be replaced. Do not try to repair it.

Go to next page for installation of float ball [3] and adjustment of arm [2].

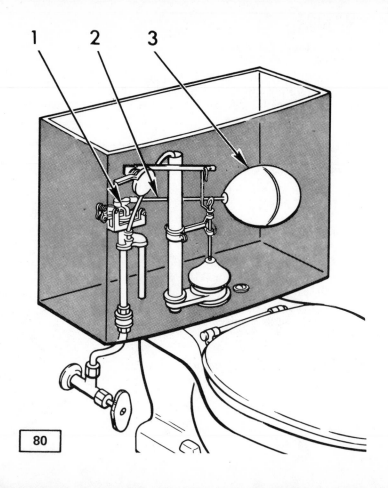

PLUMBING

Toilets — Float Ball

5. Place float ball [5] on arm [2] by turning clockwise.

6. Carefully bend the right half of arm [2] until float ball [5] is approximately 1/2-inch lower.

7. Flush toilet. Check that water shuts off approximately 1-inch below top of overflow tube [1].

Repeat steps 6 and 7 until water shuts off approximately 1-inch below top of tube [1].

8. Carefully place top [3] on tank [4].

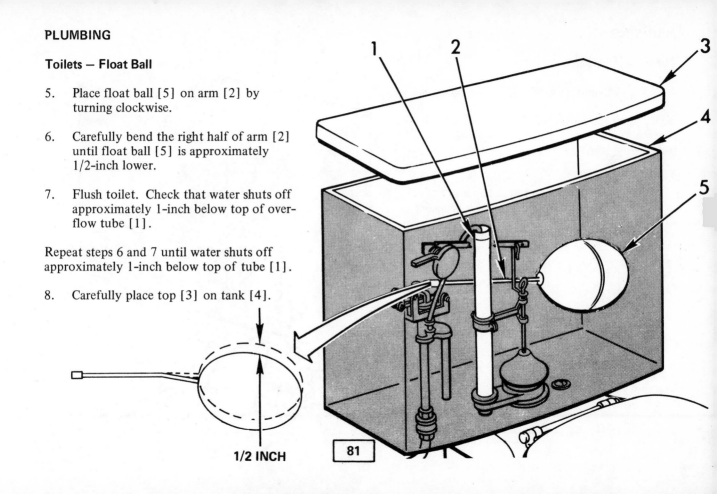

1/2 INCH

81

PLUMBING

Toilets — Inlet Valve

1. Turn off shutoff valve [5], if you have one.

If you don't have a shutoff valve [5], the next step shows the easiest method of shutting off water while making repairs to your toilet.

2. Bend coat hanger [3] over top of tank [1]. Place hook [4] around float ball arm [2]. Bend hook to keep arm at highest position.

3. Flush toilet to empty water from tank [1].

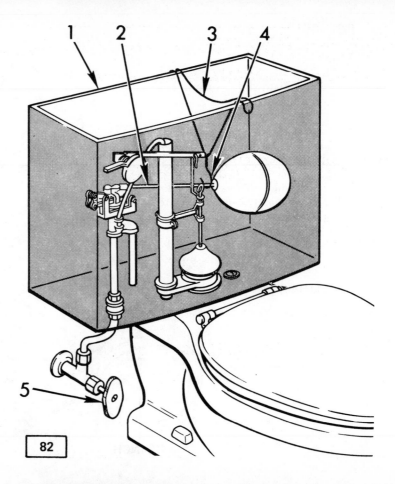

82

PLUMBING

Toilets — Inlet Valve

Inlet valve [7] may not closely resemble illustration; however, most valves in use today are removed in the same manner.

If inlet valve [7] in your tank is in a sealed unit, entire valve assembly [9] must be replaced by a plumber.

4.   Remove two screws [4] in linkage arm [3].

5.   Lift inlet valve [7] out.

6.   Check that washers [8] are not damaged.

If washers [8] are damaged, take inlet valve [7] to hardware store to insure exact replacement of washers.

7.   Place inlet valve [7] on linkage arm [3]. Place arm in position on bracket [5]. Install two screws [4].

8.   Turn on shutoff valve [6] or remove coat hanger. Carefully place top [1] on tank [2].

9.   Flush toilet.

If toilet water still does not shut off, a plumber should be called.

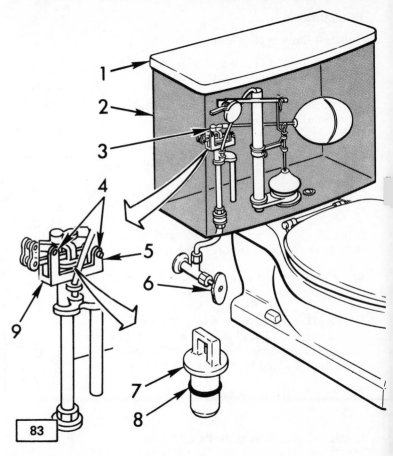

83

PLUMBING

Toilets — Slow or No Flush

1. Remove top [1] of tank [2]. Place top where it will not be damaged.

2. Check that refill tube [3] has not fallen out of overflow tube [6].

If refill tube [3] is not in overflow tube [6], carefully bend refill tube [3] until it stays inside overflow tube [6].

3. Check that handle [5] is not loose.

If handle [5] is loose, hold handle and tighten nut [4] on inside of tank [2] with wrench.

4. Check that lift wire [7] is not loose or unscrewed from flush ball [8].

If wire [7] is loose or unscrewed, tighten flush ball [8] to wire. If ball will not stay tight, ball and wire must be replaced. After replacement, go to Page 86, Step 16 to adjust lift wire.

5. Check that connecting wire [9] is not broken.

If wire [9] is broken, go to Page 86, Step 12.

6. Flush toilet.

If flush ball [8] drops before most of water is emptied from tank, continue on next page.

7. Place top [1] on tank [2].

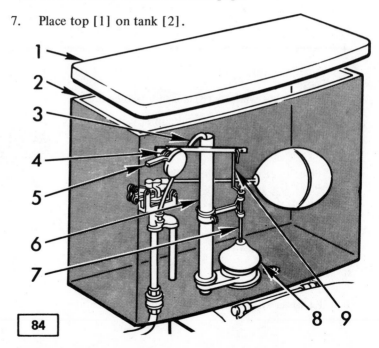

PLUMBING

Toilets — Slow or No Flush

If flush ball [7] is supported by chain [6], perform Steps 8, 9 and 10 to adjust length of chain.

If flush ball [4] is supported by wire [3], go to Page 86, Step 16 to adjust lift wire.

8. Disconnect chain [6] from trip arm [5]. Shorten chain until it reaches from trip arm to flush ball [7] with only slight amount of slack.

9. Connect chain [6] to trip arm [5].

10. Flush toilet. Check that toilet flushes correctly.

If toilet still does not flush correctly, repeat Steps 8, 9 and 10.

11. Carefully place top [1] on tank [2].

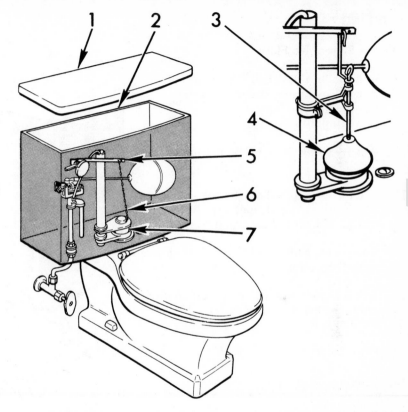

PLUMBING

Toilets — Slow or No Flush

12. While holding flush ball [8], remove lift wire [7] by turning counterclockwise. Remove lift wire from guide [6]. Leave flush ball in position.

13. Remove broken wire [4] from trip arm [3] and lift wire [7].

14. Insert lift wire [7] through hook in new connecting wire [4] and guide [6]. Bend connecting wire up and through trip arm [3].

15. While holding lift wire [7], install flush ball [8] by turning counterclockwise.

16. Adjust bend in wire [4] so hook on bottom end is about 1/4-inch below hook [5] in lift wire [7].

17. Flush toilet.

18. Carefully place top [1] on tank [2].

If toilet still does not flush correctly, a plumber should be called.

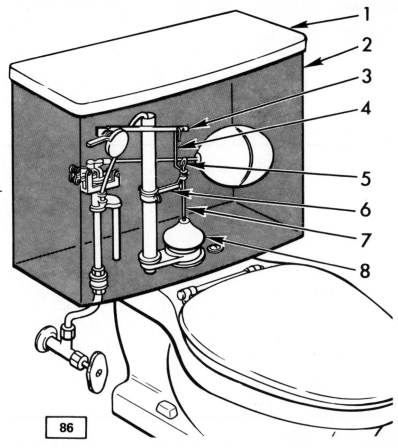

86

PLUMBING

Toilets — Inlet Pipe Leak

If toilet has no shutoff valve, main shutoff valve must be turned off. Page 38.

1. Turn off shutoff valve [3].

2. Remove top [1] of tank [7].

3. Flush toilet. Using sponge or cloth, remove all water from tank [7]. Place several rags around inlet pipe [4] where it enters tank [7].

One nut is inside tank and one is outside.

4. Loosen two nuts [5] with wrench by turning nut inside tank counterclockwise and nut outside tank clockwise.

In next step, if washer [2] will not come out easily, slightly lift ballcock assembly [6].

5. Remove washer [2]. Install a new washer. Tighten nuts [5] by turning inside nut clockwise and outside nut counterclockwise until snug.

6. Carefully place top [1] on tank [7].

7. Turn on shutoff valve [3] or main shutoff valve. Page 38.

If tank still leaks between inlet pipe [4] and tank, a plumber should be called.

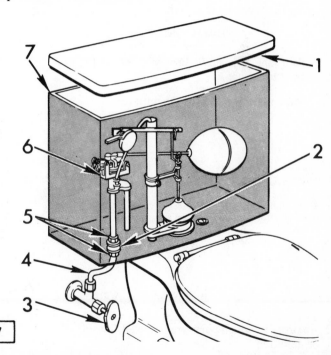

PLUMBING

Toilets — Tank Leak

Water on floor under tank [1] may indicate that nuts [4], screws [2], and washers [3] holding tank to toilet [5] are loose or corroded. They must be tightened or replaced.

CAUTION

Porcelain tank [1] can be broken if screws [2] are tightened too much.

1. Wipe area around nut [4] until dry.

2. While holding nut [4], tighten screws [2]. Check for leak.

If leak continues, nut [4], screw [2], and washers [3] must be replaced. Continue on.

If toilet has no shutoff valve [6], main shutoff valve must be turned off. Page 38.

3. Turn off shutoff valve [6].

4. Flush toilet.

5. Using sponge or cloth, remove all water from tank [1].

Note order in which parts are removed for aid in installation.

6. Using screwdriver and wrench, remove nut [4], screw [2], and washers [3].

7. Take nut [4], screw [2], and washers [3] to hardware store or plumbing shop for exact replacement.

8. Install new nut [4], screw [2], and washers [3].

9. Place top on tank.

10. Turn on shutoff valve [6] or main shutoff valve. Page 38.

If tank still leaks, a plumber should be called.

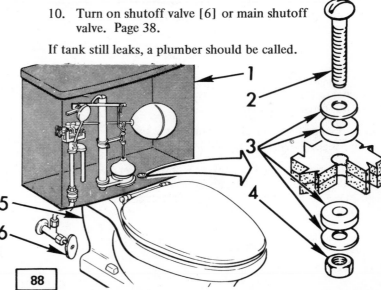

88

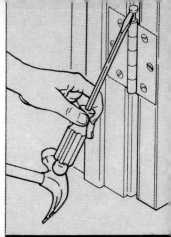

CARPENTRY

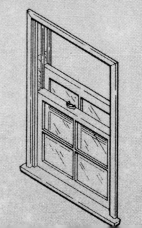

CARPENTRY

Sticking Door Locks

To correct sticking door locks you will need a clean cloth and graphite or lock lubricant.

In time, the original grease inside the lock assembly may become gummed up by dirt and dust, resulting in slow response or improper operation.

1. Turn handle [2] until latch [4] is all the way in. Hold handle in this position.

2. Apply light coat of lubricant between stationary collar [1] and shaft [3]. Repeat this step for other side of door.

3. Release handle [2].

4. Using cloth, wipe old grease and dirt from latch [4].

5. Apply light coat of lubricant to latch [4].

6. Using a cloth, wipe excess lubricant from around latch [4] and handle [2].

If door lock is equipped with lever [5], go to Page 92.

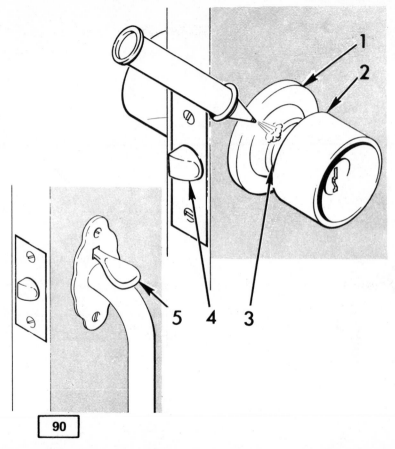

CARPENTRY

Sticking Door Locks

<u>CAUTION</u>

Lubricant should not be applied in lock keyway [2]. Lock tumblers must exert a certain amount of friction to work latch [1]. Lubricant will gather dirt and restrict proper operation of tumblers.

7. Apply light coat of lubricant to door key.

8. Insert key in keyway [2]. Operate key several times.

9. Using a cloth, wipe excess lubricant from keyway [2] and key.

10. Operate door lock several times.

If door lock still sticks, door lock mechanism must be overhauled or replaced. Call a locksmith in your area.

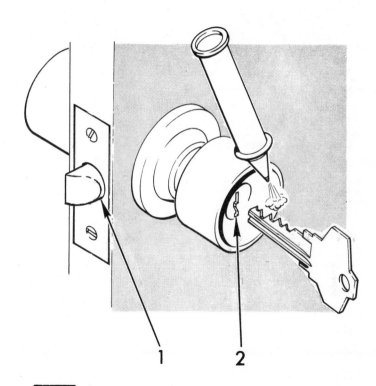

1   **2**

CARPENTRY

Sticking Door Locks

11. Press and hold lever [2].

12. Apply a light coat of lubricant to opening between lever [2] and lock body [1].

13. Operate lever [2] several times.

14. Using cloth, wipe excess lubricant from around lever [2] and lock body [1].

If latch [3] still sticks, lever and latch mechanism must be overhauled. Call a locksmith in your area.

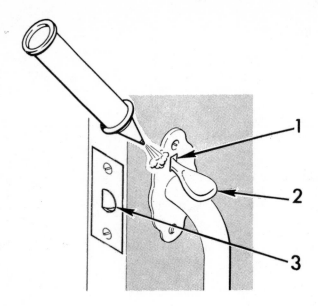

CARPENTRY

Squeaking Door

To correct a squeaking door, you will need
penetrating oil, cloth, common screwdriver,
hammer and steel wool.

1. Using common screwdriver and hammer,
    gently lift hinge pin [1] approximately
    1-inch.

2. While holding cloth under pin [1], apply
    light coat of penetrating oil to hinge [2]
    and pin.

3. Open and close door several times.

If door has stopped squeaking, install hinge
pin [1] by gently tapping down on pin with
hammer.

If door still squeaks, hinge pin [1] may be rusty.
Go to next step.

4. Using common screwdriver and hammer,
    gently tap up on hinge pin [1] to remove.

5. Using steel wool, clean rust from hinge
    pin [1].

6. Apply thin coat of lubricating oil to
    hinge pin [1].

7. Align hinge plates [2]. Install hinge
    pin [1] by gently tapping down on
    pin with hammer.

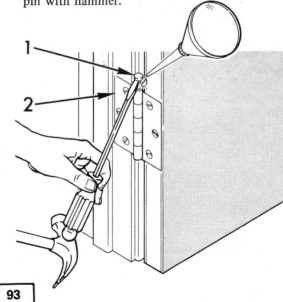

CARPENTRY

Sticking Door

To correct a sticking door you will need either
a Phillips or common screwdriver and a piece of
light cardboard or thick paper.

Changes in weather will sometimes cause door to
be difficult to open and close. Another common
cause is loose hinges. If you have small young-
sters at home who hang and swing on doors,
remember that hinges were not designed for
such punishment.

1.   Open door until you have easy access
     to hinges [2].

2.   Tighten all loose hinge screws [1].

If loose hinge screws cannot be tightened
because screw holes are worn, go to Page 98.

3.   Open and close door.

If door still sticks, go to next page.

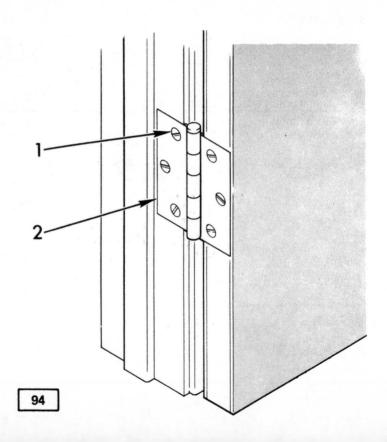

CARPENTRY

Sticking Door

To locate the place where door is sticking, inspect frame and edges of door for worn spots. If worn spots cannot be found, locate the place where the door is sticking as follows:

4. Insert a piece of paper [4] between door and frame.

5. While moving paper [4] along top, bottom and front of door, observe where door touches frame or floor.

If door sticks on top edge [7], sticking may be eliminated by installing pieces of cardboard under top hinge [1]. Page 96.

If door sticks on bottom edge [5], sticking may be eliminated by installing pieces of cardboard under bottom hinge [2]. Page 96.

If door sticks on front edge [6], top edge [8] or bottom edge [3], sticking may be eliminated by sanding or planing edge.

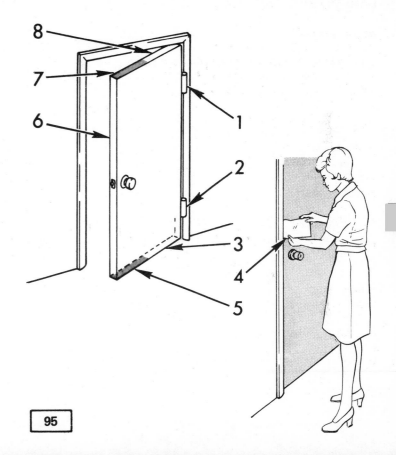

95

CARPENTRY

Sticking Door

To prevent damage to door while hinge plate is being removed, a wedge shaped scrap of wood should be used.

6. Open door. Support door at bottom with wedge shaped piece of wood [5].

7. Remove screws [1] from hinge plate [2].

8. Move hinge plate [2] away from door [4].

9. Place layer of cardboard [3] behind hinge plate [2]. Hold cardboard and hinge plate against door [4]. Install screws [1].

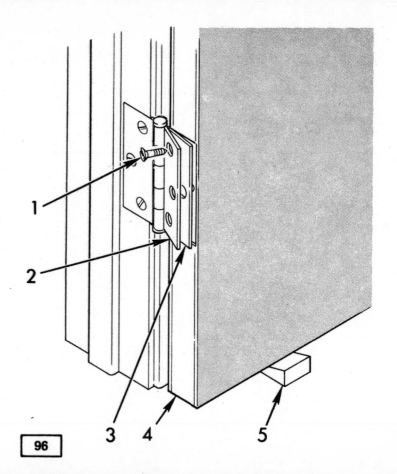

CARPENTRY

Sticking Door

10. Remove wedge [1] from under door.

11. Check that door does not stick or bind.

If door still sticks or binds, additional cardboard may be required. Repeat Steps 6 through 11.

If door still sticks after installing several pieces of cardboard under hinge, sticking edge of door must be sanded or planed.

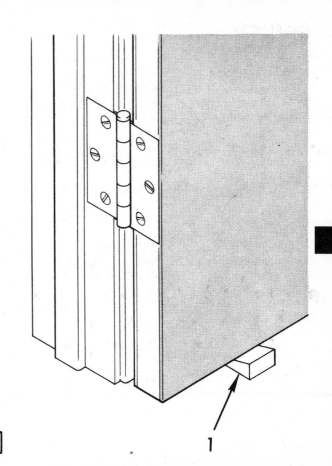

1

CARPENTRY

Worn Screw Holes

To correct worn screw holes, you will need a wedge shaped scrap of wood, hammer, common or Phillips screwdriver, wood matchsticks or pegs, and woodworking glue.

The easiest way to repair a worn out, oversize screw hole is to drive wooden matchsticks into hole. This method is best suited for lightweight doors.

The strongest and most durable method of repair is to drive a wooden peg into screw hole.

1. Open door until you have easy access to hinges [1].

2. Secure door at bottom with wedge shaped piece of wood [2].

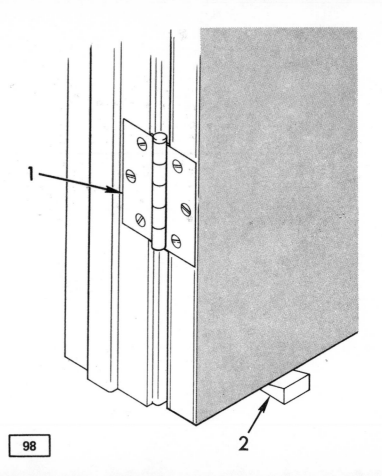

CARPENTRY

Worn Screw Holes

3. Locate and mark worn out screw hole.

4. Remove hinge screws [1]. Move hinge plate [2] away from frame [3] or door [7].

5. Apply glue to wood matchsticks [4] or peg [6]. Insert matchsticks or peg into screw hole [5].

6. Tap matchsticks [4] or peg [6] into screw hole [5] until firmly seated.

Allow a few minutes for glue to dry. Trim peg [6] or matchsticks [4] even with surface of door or frame.

7. Place hinge plate [2] against frame [3] or door [7]. Install screws [1].

8. Remove wedge [8] from under door.

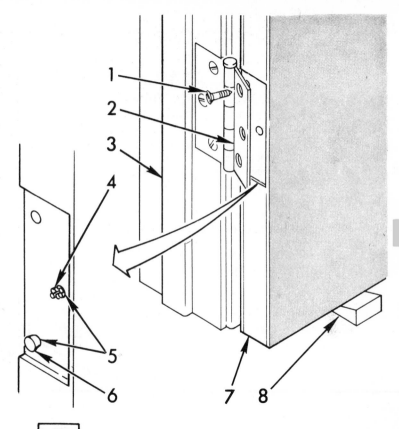

CARPENTRY

Sticking Windows and Drawers

To correct sticking windows and drawers, you will need general purpose oil, paraffin wax, soap or graphite lubricant.

For windows with metal sashes [1], clean sash with steel wool. Apply a light coat of general purpose oil to sash sliding surfaces.

For windows with wooden sashes [1], apply a light coat of paraffin wax, soap or graphite lubricant to sash sliding surfaces.

For sticking drawers, apply a light coat of paraffin wax, soap or graphite lubricant to sliding surfaces [2].

If these steps do not correct your problem, a carpenter may have to be called.

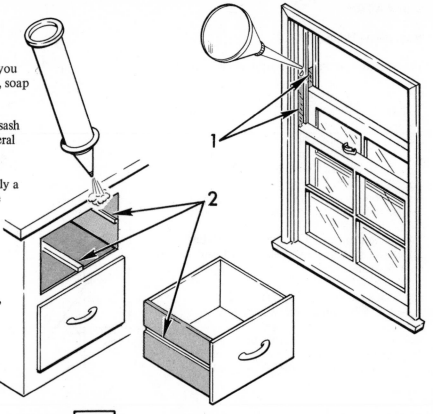

CARPENTRY

Screen Holes

For a temporary fix in your screen, you will need a small can of shellac, brush, mosquito netting or cheesecloth and scissors.

Door and window screens that are split or torn from their frames can be repaired.

Rescreening kits are available at your local hardware store in various types of screen materials, such as brass, aluminum, and nylon. These kits provide all necessary equipment to rescreen a door or window.

Although the repair in this section is only temporary, it will stop insects from entering damaged area of screen.

1.   Cut damaged area of screen into square shape.

2.   Cut mosquito netting or cheesecloth one to two-inches larger than screen hole [1].

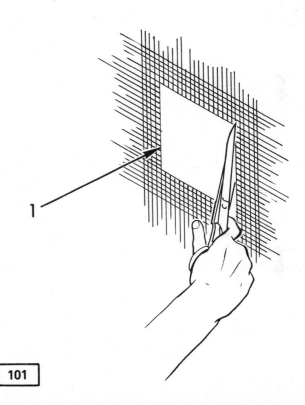

CARPENTRY

Screen Holes

3. Apply thin coat of shellac to inside and outside edge of screen [2].

4. Place netting [1] or cheesecloth over screen hole. Allow shellac to dry before continuing.

5. Apply two coats of shellac to front side of netting [1] or cheesecloth along overlapped area of screen [2].

6. Allow shellac to dry before continuing.

7. Apply thin coat of shellac to entire surface of netting [1].

The purpose of emergency medical aid is to help you save a life or prevent further injury to someone until medical help can be obtained.

It is important that you keep calm and take proper action. Knowledge of what to do will help you on both counts.

The most serious first aid emergencies that you are likely to face, where minutes count, are severe bleeding, poisoning, stoppage of breathing. Spend a few minutes learning and practicing what to do.

WARNING

The instructions in this section are not cures. They are to be used only in an emergency when professional medical assistance is not immediately available. In all cases, call for professional medical assistance when emergencies occur.

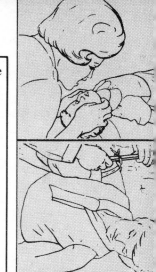

EMERGENCY MEDICAL AID

EMERGENCY MEDICAL AID

Emergency Phone Numbers

Telephone number of:

Fire Department _____

Police Department _____

Nearest Emergency Hospital _____

Family Doctor _____

Specialists: _____

_____

_____

Medical data for each member of household		
Name	Blood Type	Medical Information*
_____	_____	_____
_____	_____	_____
_____	_____	_____
_____	_____	_____
_____	_____	_____
_____	_____	_____
_____	_____	_____

More than 4 million accidents in the home result in over 26 thousand deaths every year.

*Diabetes, hemophilia, allergies, other special medical problems.

EMERGENCY MEDICAL AID

How to Place an Emergency Call

If you do not know whom to call, dial 0 for your operator. She is trained to get help for you.

In making an emergency call, be sure that you describe the kind of emergency (severe bleeding, heart attack) and the urgency for immediate aid.

MESSAGE (Fill in all blanks)

Hello, this is (your name) _____.

We have had an (injury, poisoning, heart attack, etc.).

My address is _____.

The nearest cross streets are _____.

My phone number is _____.

Please send an ambulance.

Please repeat my address and phone number.

BLEEDING

In case of severe bleeding, it is essential to first stop the bleeding, then get medical assistance.

Three First Aid methods for stopping bleeding are:

Direct Pressure Method

Pressure Point Method

Tourniquet Method

1. Direct Pressure Method. In this method, pressure is applied directly on the wound itself. Direct pressure on the wound will usually control the flow of blood. Always consider the Direct Pressure Method first. However, if severe bleeding continues, it will be necessary to use the Pressure Point Method or the Tourniquet Method.

2. Pressure Point Method. This method is used for stopping arterial bleeding (blood is bright red and spurting) from arms and legs. In this method, pressure is applied directly to the artery supplying blood to the arm or leg. The pressure point in an arm or leg is generally found where the artery crosses a bone or ligament near the surface of the body. By pressing the artery against the bone or ligament, it can be easily shut off, and bleeding will stop almost immediately.

In severe arterial bleeding, it is important that you locate the pressure point within seconds. Therefore, practice locating the pressure points now so that you will find them instantly in an emergency. Page 108.

If severe bleeding cannot be stopped quickly by the Direct Pressure Method or Pressure Point Method, you should use a tourniquet.

3. Tourniquet Method. This method consists of stopping blood flow to and from the limb by tying a band between the wound and the heart. There are differences of opinion among medical authorities regarding the use of a tourniquet. Improperly used, a tourniquet can cause severe damage to a limb and can induce or aggravate shock. However, when severe bleeding from an arm or leg can not be stopped within seconds by the Direct Pressure Method or the Pressure Point Method, a tourniquet may be your only chance to save a life. Page 110.

EMERGENCY MEDICAL AID

Bleeding

Direct Pressure Method

1. Make pad of clean cloth, handkerchief or clothing.

2. Place pad on wound.

3. Elevate wound, if possible.

4. Press and hold pad until bleeding stops. Do not be afraid to press firmly.

If bleeding does not stop, and while holding direct pressure on wound, try PRESSURE POINT METHOD, Page 108.

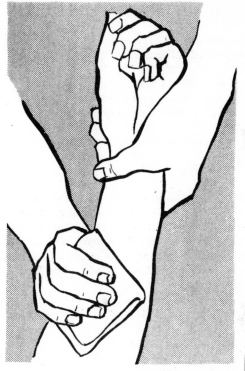

PRESSURE POINT METHOD

EMERGENCY MEDICAL AID

Pressure Point Method

Bleeding from Arm

Pressure point is located on inside of upper arm near armpit (see illustration). Once you find pressure point and apply pressure to it, bleeding from artery should stop immediately. To apply pressure at pressure point:

1. Press fingers firmly against large bone on inside of upper arm. Check that bleeding stops immediately. Continue applying pressure.

2. Lift arm above body, if possible.

4. Place victim on his back with head lower than feet, if possible.

5. Request someone cover victim with blanket.

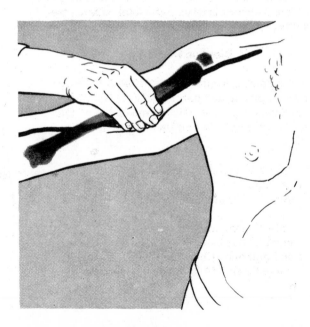

EMERGENCY MEDICAL AID

Pressure Point Method

WARNING

If you cannot locate pressure point within five to ten seconds, use Tourniquet Method since bleeding from a severed artery can be fatal within a few minutes.

Bleeding from Leg

Pressure point is located on groin about halfway between hipbone and pubic bone (see illustration) near inguinal ligament. This ligament can be felt as a firm cord extending from hipbone to pubic bone.

Once you find pressure point and apply pressure to it, bleeding from the artery should stop immediately. To apply pressure at pressure point:

1. Press fingers firmly in area just below ligament, about halfway between pubic bone and hipbone. Check that bleeding stops immediately. Continue applying pressure.

2. Lift leg above body, if possible.

3. Place victim on his back with head lower than feet, if possible.

4. Request someone cover victim with blanket.

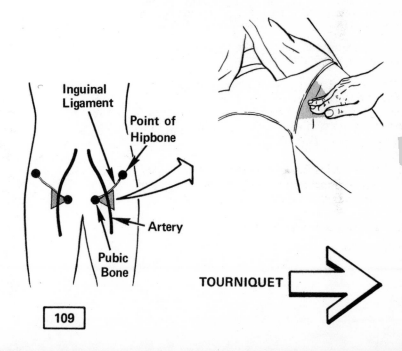

EMERGENCY MEDICAL AID

Tourniquet Method

WARNING

Tourniquet should be used only when bleeding from artery in arm or leg can not be stopped by Direct Pressure Method or Pressure Point Method.

Tourniquet should be released for ten seconds every five to ten minutes.

Locate tourniquet on fleshy part of limb, as close to wound as possible.

1. Tie handkerchief, belt, stocking or other wide band loosely on limb between heart and wound.

2. Place stick or rod between knot and flesh.

3. Twist stick just until bleeding stops.

4. Loosen tourniquet for ten seconds once every five to ten minutes — even if bleeding starts again.

If bleeding stops, leave tourniquet in position to use, but do not tighten

5. If possible, place victim on his back with head lower than feet.

6. Cover victim with blanket.

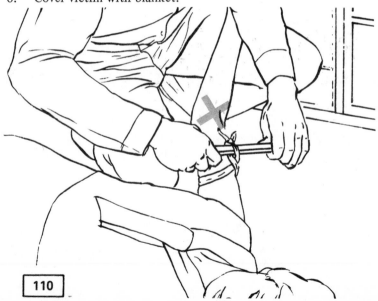

EMERGENCY MEDICAL AID

Nose Bleed

If nose bleeding cannot be stopped, call for medical aid. Severe or prolonged nose bleeding can result in large loss of blood.

1. Using fingers, squeeze just under bridge of nose.

2. Tilt head back if bleeding is not severe.

3. Keep victim quiet.

4. Apply ice around area of nose.

5. Place cotton deep into nose.

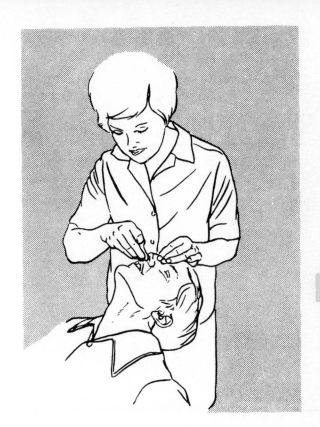

EMERGENCY MEDICAL AID

Burns

There are three degrees of burns:

First Degree — Mildest burn of the three, producing redness and mild pain.

Second Degree — Burn reddens and blisters skin. Severe pain may be present.

Third Degree — Burn destroys skin and may char area of burn. Pain may not be felt due to destruction of nerve endings in area of burn.

There is great danger of infection due to burns. All but the most minor burns should be seen by a physician.

First Degree Burn

1. Gently wash burned area with mild soapy solution. Do not use detergent.

2. Cover burn with gauze or simple dressing if small area is involved.

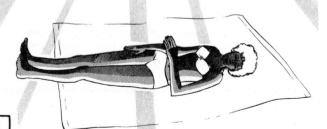

Burns

Second and Third Degree Burns

WARNING

Do not pull clothing away from burn. Instead, cut clothing away from area surrounding burn. Do not remove clothing that is directly on burn.

Do not pull debris or pieces of clothing out of the burn.

Do not break blisters or touch burned area.

Do not apply butter or any medication to the burn.

In cases of third degree burns with large, open wounds, cover burn with clean or sterile bandage and wait for medical assistance.

1. Carefully remove clothing in vicinity of burned area.

2. Gently apply a solution of soapy lukewarm water to burn.

3. Keep burned area wet with lukewarm soapy solution until medical assistance arrives.

4. Keep victim calm and warm.

5. Place victim on his back with head lower than feet, if possible.

EMERGENCY MEDICAL AID

Choking

Do not slap someone on the back at the first sign of choking. Let him try to cough out the obstruction first. Choking and coughing are nature's way of removing any blockage from the windpipe.

If the person cannot clear the obstruction, you must help.

If he can breathe, call for immediate medical assistance.

If the person cannot breathe, apply artificial respiration. Page 118.

Aid for Small Children

1. Hold child upside down and slap him sharply between the shoulder blades several times.

WARNING

When removing an obstruction from a child's mouth, be very careful not to push the obstruction further down his throat.

2. Reach finger into child's mouth and try to remove obstruction if the choking does not stop.

3. Call for immediate medical assistance if choking cannot be stopped.

4. If breathing stops or child turns blue, apply artificial respiration. Page 118.

AID FOR
ADULTS

Choking

Aid for Adults

WARNING

Do not give victim liquids. Do not induce vomiting.

1. Place victim face down on bed or sofa.

2. Allow victim's head to hang over the edge.

3. Slap victim sharply between the shoulder blades several times.

4. Reach finger into victim's mouth and try to remove obstruction if choking does not stop.

5. Call for immediate medical assistance if choking cannot be stopped.

6. If breathing stops or victim turns blue, apply artificial respiration. Page 118.

EMERGENCY MEDICAL AID

Heart Attacks

When the first signs of a heart attack appear, immediately get the victim to an emergency hospital. If this is not possible, call for medical assistance.

WARNING

Call a physician even if victim thinks he is going to feel better in a few minutes.

SYMPTOMS

Pain in the upper abdomen, chest, — may be extending into the arms or neck.

Shortness of breath.

Nausea, vomiting and sweating in combination with above symptoms.

1. Place victim in comfortable reclining position.

2. Loosen clothing.

3. Keep victim calm.

4. Cover victim with a blanket.

If breathing stops, apply artificial respiration. Page 118.

If the victim loses consciousness, his heart may have stopped.

You may try to stimulate the heart by striking his chest with several sharp blows just to the left side of his breastbone.

If victim is still not breathing, apply artificial respiration. Page 118.

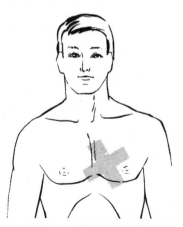

EMERGENCY MEDICAL AID

Drowning

1. Place victim's head much lower than feet to
    let water out of chest.

2. Turn victim's head to one side to prevent
    vomit from entering lungs.

3. If victim is not breathing or turns blue,
    apply artificial respiration. Page 118.

4. Keep victim warm.

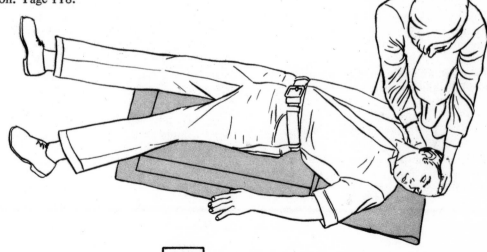

EMERGENCY MEDICAL AID

Artificial Respiration

Being familiar with these procedures may help
you save a life. They have saved many victims of
DROWNING, SUFFOCATION, and ELECTRI-
CAL SHOCK.

Even though a person has stopped breathing, he
may still be alive.

If artificial respiration is started IMMEDIATELY,
you may save that person's life by keeping him
breathing until medical assistance arrives.

Do not leave a victim alone. Have someone call
for help while you apply artificial respiration.

Don't give up! It may take some time for the
victim to start breathing in a normal manner.

Stop artificial respiration only after breathing
becomes normal or until a physician or rescue
personnel tells you to stop.

WARNING

**When removing an obstruction from victim's
mouth, be careful not to push the obstruction
further down his throad.**

Artificial respiration techniques for infants and
children up to five years old are slightly different
from those for older children and adults. When
applying artificial respiration to an infant or a
child under five, proceed as follows:

1. Cover the infant's nose and mouth with
    your mouth.

2. Do not blow too hard into the infant's lungs.
    Injury could result from overexpansion
    of lungs.

ARTIFICIAL
RESPIRATION
TECHNIQUES

EMERGENCY MEDICAL AID

Artificial Respiration for Infant (under five years old)

1. Remove all foreign matter from infant's mouth.

2. Place infant on his back.

3. Place fingers under angle of jaw.

4. Carefully pull head back lifting chin as high as possible. Hold head back.

This alone may start infant's breathing again. Be sure breathing is normal.

5. Open infant's mouth.

6. Cover his mouth AND nose with your mouth.

WARNING

Do not blow too hard into infant's lungs. You may injure infant's lungs by overexpanding them.

7. Blow into infant's mouth and nose. Use short puffs of air. Use only enough force to expand infant's chest.

8. Remove your mouth to allow air to escape from infant's lungs.

If air does not escape from infant's mouth, check position of head or tongue. Check for obstructions in mouth.

9. Repeat Steps 7 and 8 once every three seconds until infant starts to breathe in a NORMAL manner.

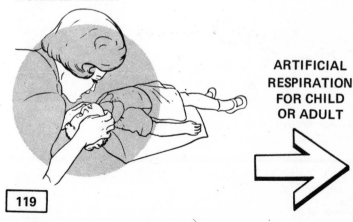

ARTIFICIAL RESPIRATION FOR CHILD OR ADULT

EMERGENCY MEDICAL AID

Artificial Respiration for Child or Adult

Artificial respiration for infant (under five years old). Page 119.

If possible, remove clothing from chest so that movement of chest can be observed.

1. Remove all foreign matter, including false teeth, from mouth.

2. Place victim on back.

3. Place fingers under angle of jaw using both hands.

4. Pull head back, lifting chin up as high as possible.

This alone may start person breathing again. Be sure breathing is normal.

5. Pinch and hold victim's nostrils together using thumbs.

6. Open victim's mouth. Cover his mouth with your mouth.

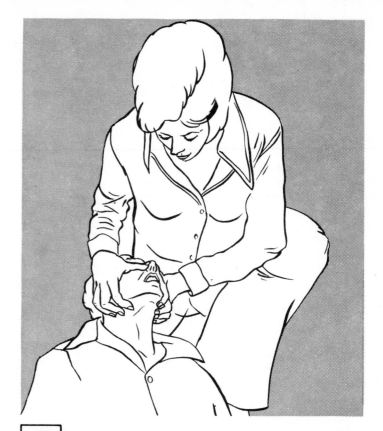

EMERGENCY MEDICAL AID

Artificial Respiration for Child or Adult

7. Blow air into victim's mouth until you see his chest expand.

8. Remove your mouth. Allow air to escape from victim's lungs.

There must be an exchange of air. After forcing air into victim, listen for air escaping from his lungs. If no air is exchanged, pull tongue forward using cloth to aid in holding tongue. Check for obstructions.

9. Repeat Steps 7 and 8 once every five seconds until victim starts to breathe in a NORMAL manner.

If victim still has not started to breathe, his heart may have stopped. You may try to stimulate the heart by striking his chest several sharp blows just to the left side of his breastbone.

Repeat entire artificial respiration procedure.

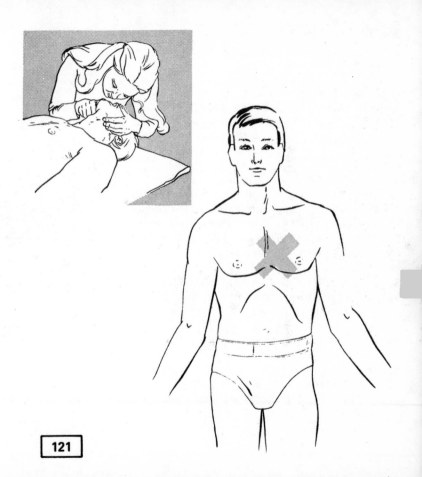

EMERGENCY MEDICAL AID

Convulsions — Adult

Most convulsions will stop within 5 minutes.
Do not be alarmed if victim looses control of
bladder or bowels during the convulsion.
The main objective of aid is to prevent the victim
from injuring himself during convulsions.

To prevent victim from biting his tongue, some
object should be placed in his mouth. This object
should be soft enough not to break his teeth and
large enough so that he cannot choke on it or
swallow it. A wallet or rolled up handkerchief is
handy and ideal for this purpose.

1. Place wallet, rolled up handkerchief, or soft
    object in person's mouth to prevent him
    from biting his tongue.

2. Place person on his back in protected area to
    prevent injury.

3. Check that person continues breathing.
    If breathing stops, apply aritifical respiration.
    Page 118.

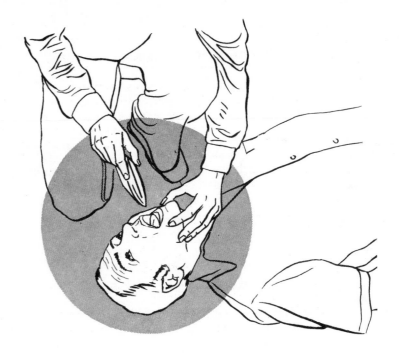

EMERGENCY MEDICAL AID

Unconsciousness

1. Check breathing. If breathing stops, apply artificial respiration. Page 118.

2. Turn victim's head to one side, if possible without injuring him.

3. Place victim on his back with head lower than feet.

4. Keep victim warm.

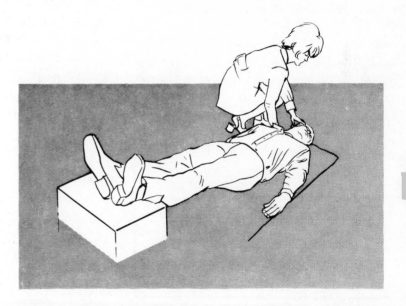

EMERGENCY MEDICAL AID

Fainting

Fainting may be caused by physical disturbances, as well as emotional reactions. Therefore, call your physician in any case of fainting.

SYMPTOMS

Complaints of weakness, dizziness or spots before the eyes.

Pale or sweaty appearance.

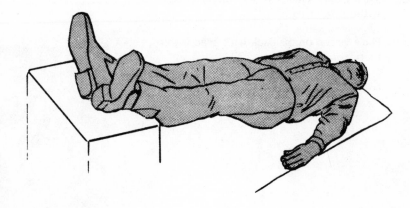

1. Place victim on his back with head lower than feet.

2. Loosen clothing and keep warm.

WARNING

Do not give victim any liquids or food.

3. Have victim rest for at least 15 minutes.

Fractures

Open Fracture (Bone Exposed)

WARNING

Request medical assistance immediately.

1. Stop bleeding. Page 106.

2. Allow victim to place fractured area in position that is most comfortable, if necessary.

3. Cover wound with clean gauze.

WARNING

Be sure that splint does not directly touch bone.

4. Apply splint or wrap fracture to prevent movement of broken bone and adjacent joints.

5. Place victim on his back.

6. Cover victim with blanket.

Closed Fracture

1. Allow victim to place fractured area in position that is most comfortable, if necessary.

2. Apply splint or wrap fracture to prevent movement of broken bone and adjacent joints.

3. Cover victim with blanket.

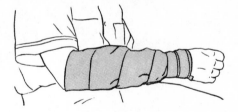

Insect Bites and Stings

Most insect bites are not serious unless there is an allergic reaction. The exceptions are scorpions and black widow spiders. Page 127.

If there is any doubt as to what type of insect has bitten you, see your physician. If possible, catch insect and place it in bottle.

1. Remove stinger, if still in skin.

2. Apply ice to area of bite.

3. Apply a thick paste made of baking soda and water to area of bite.

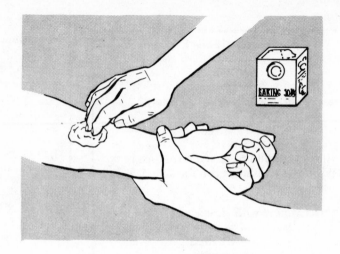

BLACK WIDOW SPIDER BITES AND SCORPION STINGS.

EMERGENCY MEDICAL AID

Black Widow Spider Bites and Scorpion Stings

WARNING

Get the victim to an emergency hospital immediately. If you cannot transport the victim to a hospital, call for medical assistance.

Black widow bites and scorpion stings are rarely fatal to adults but the victim should receive medical aid.

SYMPTOMS

Swelling and redness.

Victim may experience a spreading, burning pain in the area of the bite.

Victim may experience stomach pain, nausea and vomiting.

Victim may have a fever and severe headache.

1. Place victim on his back.

2. Keep victim calm. Do not allow victim to walk or move any more than absolutely necessary.

3. Cover victim with blanket.

4. Apply ice to area of bite.

Red Hourglass on Underside of Body.

EMERGENCY MEDICAL AID

Snake Bites

WARNING

Get the victim to an emergency hospital immediately. If you cannot transport the victim to a hospital, call for medical assistance.

There are very few deaths in the United States due to snake bites. Approximately 2% of all poisonous snake bites are fatal.

It is not always possible to tell whether a bite was inflicted by a poisonous snake or a non-poisonous snake. Generally, a person bitten by a poisonous snake will experience the symptoms listed in this section.

If possible to do so without endangering yourself and others, it is best to kill the snake and keep it for identification. Positive identification will help the physician determine correct treatment.

SYMPTOMS

Victim will usually experience immediate pain in the area of bite.

Area of bite will usually swell and become purple in color.

Victim may feel weak and have trouble breathing.

Pulse may become weak.

Victim may faint or vomit.

SNAKE BITE TREATMENT

TREATMENT

There is some disagreement among medical authorities regarding the effectiveness of making incisions in the wound to remove venom.

If medical assistance will not be readily available, you may consider carrying a snake bite kit. Follow the manufacturer's instructions for use.

In all cases of snake bite, apply the following treatment.

1.   Keep victim still.

2.   Keep victim calm. Do not allow victim to walk or move any more than absolutely necessary.

3.   Keep victim warm.

4.   Apply ice to area of bite.

If victim was bitten in arm or leg, tie a band between wound and heart, about two inches above wound. Do not tighten band as much as a tourniquet. The purpose of the band is to retard the flow of venom toward the heart.

EMERGENCY MEDICAL AID

Animal Bites

WARNING

An animal bite may be dangerous and should be checked by a physician.

If possible to do so without endangering other people, the animal should be caught and kept until it is tested for rabies or other diseases.

Do not try to stop minor bleeding from animal bites. Bleeding will clean out the wound.

1. Wash wound thoroughly with mild soapy solution.

2. Cover wound with sterile dressing.

3. Keep person calm and warm.

EMERGENCY MEDICAL AID

Poison Oak, Ivy and Sumac

SYMPTOMS

Skin may become red and swollen.

Small blisters may appear on the skin. Blisters may become large after several hours.

Violent itching may be experienced.

WARNING

If the victim experiences a rash on a large area of the body, get medical help. Do not allow victim to scratch rash.

TREATMENT

1. Wash area thoroughly with soapy solution.

2. Small rash — apply calamine solution.

   Large rash — bathe in solution of 1 cup baking soda in bathtub of water.

If itching is not relieved, call your physician for medication.

POISON IVY
Three Leaf Cluster. Pointed Leaves.

POISON OAK
Three Leaf Cluster. Rounded Leaves.

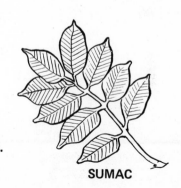

SUMAC

EMERGENCY MEDICAL AID

Poisoning

Fast action may be important in saving the life of a victim of poisoning. If at all possible, locate the container from which the poison came. All harmful substances must have a label on which the first aid treatment is written.

Get the victim to an emergency hospital immediately. Bring the poison container with you.

If you can not transport the victim to a hospital, call for medical assistance.

Use the Poison Antidote Chart for aid where container label is not available.

```
┌─────────────────────────────────────────────────────────┐
│                  Poison Antidote Chart                  │
│                                                         │
│  Section                                          Page  │
│                                                         │
│  Medicine (overdosage) . . . . . . . . . . . .    135   │
│  Household polishes and cleaners . . . . . . . .  136   │
│  Insecticides — poisonous substances — paint  . . 138   │
│  Cosmetics  . . . . . . . . . . . . . . . . . .   139   │
└─────────────────────────────────────────────────────────┘
```

More children are poisoned by eating an overdose of aspirin than any other substance.

Poisoning

Treatment by Induced Vomiting

This treatment is generally used in poisoning by drugs, barbiturates and non-corrosive substances.

WARNING

Induce vomiting only when it is recommended by a physician, container label, or in Poison Antidote Chart. Page 135.

Do not induce vomiting if victim is unconscious or having convulsions.

Keep victim's head down and turned sideways to prevent him from choking on vomit.

Vomiting can be induced by any of the following methods:

- Placing finger down throat.

- Two tablespoons of salt dissolved in glass of warm water.

- Two tablespoons of mustard dissolved in glass of warm water.

- Bathroom hand soap chips dissolved in glass of warm water. Do not use detergent.

Universal antidote (Page 134) may be given to victim after vomiting to dilute/neutralize remaining poisonous substances.

Treatment by Dilute/Neutralizer

This treatment is generally used in poisoning caused by strong acids, alkalis or corrosive substances.

This treatment does not remove poison but dilutes or neutralizes it.

An inexpensive and effective universal antidote for diluting/neutralizing poisons can be prepared from ingredients available from your druggist.

The universal antidote may be given to dilute/neutralize poisons when vomiting IS NOT TO BE INDUCED.

If in doubt between inducing vomiting or treating by dilute/neutralizer method, treat by dilute/neutralizer method.

Recipe for Universal Antidote

Mix ingredients and store in labelled container in medicine cabinet for use in emergency.

> 2 parts activated charcoal
> 1 part tannic acid
> 1 part magnesium oxide

1. Add one or two tablespoons of universal antidote to a glass of warm water.

2. Give antidote to victim.

If antidote is not available, make a solution of

> 1 part strong tea
> 1 part milk of magnesia
> 2 parts crumbled burned toast

POISON ANTIDOTE CHART

MEDICINE (overdosage)

SUBSTANCE	WHAT TO DO
Aspirin Birth Control Pills Cough Medicine Hormones	1. If victim is conscious, **INDUCE VOMITING**. Page 133.
Belladona	1. If victim is conscious, **INDUCE VOMITING**. Page 133. 2. Give victim strong tea or universal antidote.
Sleeping Pills	If victim stops breathing, apply artificial respiration. Page 118. 1. If victim is conscious, **INDUCE VOMITING**. Page 133. 2. Keep victim awake by forcing him to walk. 3. Give victim strong coffee or tea. 4. Get medical assistance immediately.
Tranquilizers	1. If victim is conscious, **INDUCE VOMITING**. Page 133. 2. Give victim 2 glasses of water, each glass containing 2 tablespoons of epsom salts.
Vitamins and Iron Tablets	1. If victim is conscious, **INDUCE VOMITING**. Page 133. 2. Give victim a glass of milk.

HOUSEHOLD POLISHES AND CLEANERS

SUBSTANCE	WHAT TO DO
Automatic dishwasher detergent Charcoal fire starter Cleaning fluid Furniture polish Gasoline Household cleaners Kerosene	**WARNING** **DO NOT INDUCE VOMITING.** 1. Give victim 3 glasses of milk or 1 glass of universal antidote.
Laundry bleach	**WARNING** **DO NOT INDUCE VOMITING.** 1. Give victim mixture of 1 ounce of olive oil, 1 banana and 1 egg white.
Fabric softeners	1. If victim is conscious, **INDUCE VOMITING.** Page 133. 2. Give victim glass of milk.

HOUSEHOLD POLISHES AND CLEANERS

SUBSTANCE	WHAT TO DO
Household ammonia	**WARNING** **DO NOT INDUCE VOMITING.** 1. Give victim 1 glass of citrus juice or 1 tablespoon of vinegar in 1 glass of water, then 2. Give victim 2 raw egg whites or 2 oz. of olive oil.
Toilet bowl and drain cleaners	**WARNING** **DO NOT INDUCE VOMITING.** **DO NOT** give bicarbonates such as baking soda. 1. Give victim 3 glasses of milk or 2 egg whites or 1 tablespoon soap in 1 glass of water or 2 ounces of milk of magnesia.
Wax remover	**WARNING** **DO NOT INDUCE VOMITING.** 1. Give victim 3 glasses of milk.

INSECTICIDES — POISON SUBSTANCES — PAINT (See label for contents)

SUBSTANCE	WHAT TO DO
Arsenic	1. If victim is conscious, **INDUCE VOMITING.** Page 133. 2. Give victim 3 glasses of milk.
DDT	1. If victim is conscious, **INDUCE VOMITING.** Page 133. 2. Give victim 2 glasses of water, each glass containing 2 tablespoons of epsom salts.
Lye	**WARNING** **DO NOT INDUCE VOMITING.** 1. Give victim 2 glasses of water, each glass containing 2 tablespoons of vinegar, then 2. Give victim 2 raw egg whites or 2 oz. of olive oil.
Paint — Dry	1. Give victim 2 glasses of milk or water. 2. If victim is conscious, **INDUCE VOMITING.** Page 133.
Paint — Liquid	**WARNING** **DO NOT INDUCE VOMITING.** 1. Give victim 3 glasses of milk or water.

COSMETICS

SUBSTANCE	WHAT TO DO
After shave lotion Cologne or perfume Hand and skin lotion Liquid makeup	1. If victim is conscious, **INDUCE VOMITING.** Page 133. 2. Give victim 3 glasses of milk.
Deodorant	1. If victim is conscious, **INDUCE VOMITING.** Page 133. 2. Give victim 2 tablespoons of milk of magnesia in a glass of water.
Bubble bath liquid Hair rinse and conditioners Shampoo	1. If victim is conscious, **INDUCE VOMITING.** Page 133. 2. Give victim 3 glasses of milk or water.
Bath oil Lacquers Nail polish and removers	1. If victim is conscious, **INDUCE VOMITING.** Page 133. 2. Give victim 3 glasses of milk.
Home permanent-wave and neutralizer solutions	1. Give victim 3 glasses of milk or water. 2. If victim is conscious, **INDUCE VOMITING.** Page 133. 3. Give victim lemonade or citrus juices.

EMERGENCY MEDICAL AID

Sprain

It is sometimes difficult to determine whether an injury is a sprain or a fracture. Medical examination may be required.

1. If possible, raise injured joint to reduce pain and swelling.

2. Periodically apply cold cloths or ice during first 6 hours after injury.

3. Apply bandage and, if injury is on wrist or elbow, apply sling.

<u>CAUTION</u>

Purpose of bandage is to keep joint from moving and to permit injured ligaments to rest. Bandage must not interfere with circulation of blood.

Be sure that bandage does not become too tight, if joint swells.

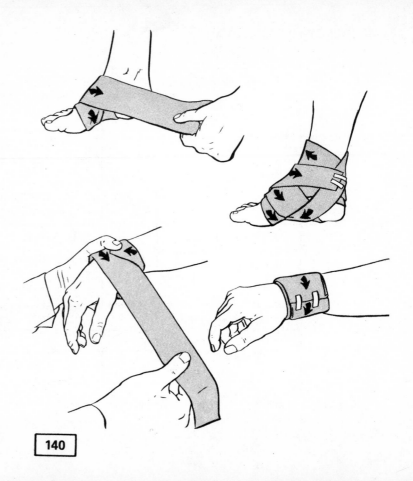

GOING AWAY ?

	Page

GOING AWAY?

Make Your Home Safe

 Whether leaving your home for a few days or for an extended period of time, enjoy your absence by leaving with a sense of security.

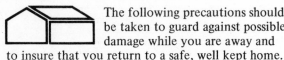 The following precautions should be taken to guard against possible damage while you are away and to insure that you return to a safe, well kept home.

When planning an absence, leave your home in the best possible condition. If your absence will be longer than a few days, it is recommended that you follow these procedures to shut off gas and utilities.

Doing so will help prevent possible fire and water damage to your home while you are away.

Electrical

 Be sure refrigerator is defrosted if shutting off power to the kitchen electrical circuit.

 If timers are used to control lights within the home, do not shut off power to those electrical circuits.

 Shut off electrical power to desired circuits at circuit breaker or fuse box.

Upon return:

 Turn on all electrical power at circuit breaker or fuse box.

GOING AWAY?

Make Your Home Safe

Water

 Shut off main water valve or call water company to do so.

 If main water valve handle can be removed, remove it to prevent tampering while you are away.

 Open all sink and outside water taps. Allow water to drain. Close all taps.

 Flush each toilet. If weather will be below freezing during your absence, pour a cup of anti-freeze in each toilet bowl.

Upon return:

 Install main water valve handle, if you removed it.

 Turn on main water valve or call water company to do so.

 Open all sink and outside water taps. Allow water to run until free of air. Close all taps.

 Flush each toilet.

Gas

 Request local gas company to shut off gas. There are considerable dangers involved in attempting to do this yourself. In most areas, this service will be free of charge.

Upon return:

 Request local gas company to turn on gas. They will gladly do so in addition to checking for leaks and proper operation of your appliances.

GOING AWAY?

Burglar-Proofing

Regardless of how long you plan to be away, it is essential that your home presents a "lived-in" look. Few burglars will tamper with an occupied home. Observe the following:

 Request your neighbor to regularly do the following to insure a "lived-in" look for your home:

 Inform a trusted neighbor of your plans. Leave a key with him. DO NOT leave a key under the doormat or other obvious hiding place.

 Remove circulars and debris.

 Do not publicize your vacation plans. Many burglars rely on newspapers, etc., for their information on vacant homes.

 Remove mail from mailbox daily (unless mail is discontinued or forwarded).

Vary the position of drapes and curtains.

 Request your neighbor not to inform strangers of your absence.

GOING AWAY?

Burglar-Proofing

 Discontinue all deliveries and services by phone or in person ahead of time. DO NOT leave notes.

 Arrange for periodic lawn care. Not only will this present a "lived-in" look, but will save you work when you return.

 Be sure to lock up all tools and ladders. Don't provide burglars with tools for doing his job.

 Adjust telephone to its lowest volume. An unanswered telephone is a sure indication of an unoccupied home.

 Your porchlight and an inside light should be set on timers or turned on by a neighbor for operation at night. Be sure timers are set properly.

 Advise the local police department of your plans. They'll be glad to check your home regularly. Be sure to inform them of your return.

 Place a stick or broom handle in tracks of sliding doors and windows to insure good security.

 Immediately before leaving, be sure that all doors, windows, and fence gates are securely locked.

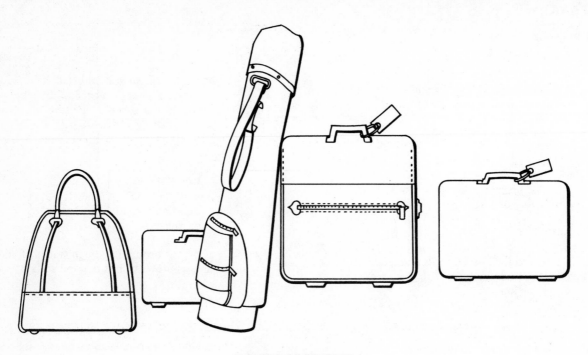

HAVE A SAFE TRIP

146

A WOMAN'S GUIDE TO SURVIVAL

A WOMAN'S GUIDE TO SURVIVAL

Walking

Police departments tell us there is an alarming increase in rate of attacks and attempted attacks on women.

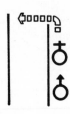

If you think you are being followed, cross to other side of street. If you are still being followed run to a lighted home or business and call police.

Three of the most dangerous things for a woman to do alone are walking, driving or being at home.

If a car approaches and driver is bothering you, run in opposite direction of car's travel. The driver will have to make a U-turn to chase you. The time this takes him may allow you to get away.

There is no such thing as a "safe" neighborhood or area. Danger may exist in the most innocent looking surroundings.

Safety hints in this section may well save your life or save you from injury.
Read them thoroughly.

Always walk near curb to avoid passing close to shrubbery, dark doorways or other places in which an attacker may hide.

Try to vary your daily routine. Do not use the same route and times every day. If you cannot vary your routine, have friends and neighbors watch for you when coming home.

If you are being followed as you approach your home, go to a neighbor's home. Do not try to get into your home. Attacker may force his way in as you open door.

When you arrive home by taxicab, ask driver to wait until you are inside house.

Always have house key ready as you approach your door. This precaution will prevent you from taking time at door to search through your purse for your house key.

Do not enter your home if anything appears even slightly suspicious. Go to a neighbor's home and call police.
A FALSE ALARM TO POLICE IS BETTER THAN YOUR BEING ATTACKED.

If you are threatened, **SCREAM AND KEEP ON SCREAMING!** Even if you are ordered to stop, your chances for survival are better if you continue screaming.

Try to knee or kick molester in the groin at your first opportunity. This will put him out of action long enough for you to run away screaming.

Driving

Always keep car doors locked. When possible, keep all car windows rolled up.

Try to travel on busy, well lighted streets.

Always leave car in gear while waiting at stop lights or pedestrian crossings. If someone tries to get into your car blow horn and drive away quickly.

Do not stop for another car even if it has flashing red lights unless it is marked police car, ambulance or fire vehicle. There have been cases of criminals stopping their victims at night by using flashing red lights. Only police officers in uniform will request you to stop your car and get out.

If you wish to help, go to nearest telephone and call for assistance. Many women are robbed or attacked because they stopped to help what appeared to be someone with car trouble.

If you are stranded in a car that will not start, stay inside and lock the doors. Do not risk being attacked. Do not get out of the car for any reason.

A WOMAN'S GUIDE TO SURVIVAL

If you think you are being followed by another car:

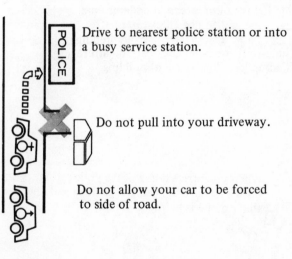

Drive to nearest police station or into a busy service station.

Do not pull into your driveway.

Do not allow your car to be forced to side of road.

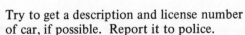

Try to get a description and license number of car, if possible. Report it to police.

If your car breaks down in an isolated area:

Raise car hood. Turn on emergency blinkers.

Sit inside car with windows up and doors locked.

Do not get out of car to talk to passersby. Momentarily open your window slightly and ask them to call for assistance.

Do not accept rides from strangers.

If another motorist indicates that your car is not working properly while driving, do not stop or get out of your car to investigate — drive to nearest service station or friend's house.

Driving (Parking)

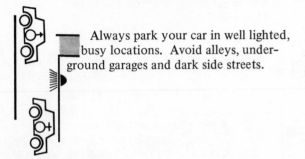

Always park your car in well lighted, busy locations. Avoid alleys, underground garages and dark side streets.

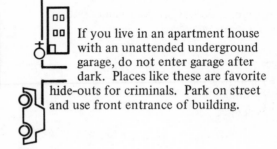

If you live in an apartment house with an unattended underground garage, do not enter garage after dark. Places like these are favorite hide-outs for criminals. Park on street and use front entrance of building.

Do not get out of car until you are sure there are no suspicious persons in area.

When you arrive home, leave your car lights on until you have opened garage door and checked that no one is hiding in garage.

Always lock your car. When you come back to your car, check that front and rear seats are unoccupied before getting into car.

A WOMAN'S GUIDE TO SURVIVAL

In The Home

If you live alone, do not list your name in telephone book or on mailbox as:

| Jane Jones | or Miss J. Jones |

This tells criminal that you are a woman living alone.

List your name:

| J. Jones |
| R. Smith |

J. Jones
Or, list two names to make it appear that you do not live alone.

When you move into a different apartment or home, be sure you have all locks changed or you will never know who else has a key to your home.

When you go out at night leave radio playing loud enough to be heard outside your door. Leave on several lights.

Never leave only the outside porch light on. This is a signal you are not home. Leave a bedroom or bathroom light on also.

If possible, avoid going into a public laundry or apartment building laundry alone at night. These are prime target areas for attackers.

If you hear a prowler or burglar in your house, get out of house through a back door or window and go to a neighbor's house to call police.

Never open door to strangers. If you are expecting repairmen, be sure they identify themselves before you let them into your house.

IMPORTANT TELEPHONE NUMBERS

The safest way to handle most emergencies is to call the appropriate person or department for experienced professional assistance.

In completing this telephone list, take the time to insure the assistance you need for any emergency is the closest available to your home.

Fire Department: _____

Police Department: _____

Doctor: Night _____

         Day _____

Ambulance: _____

Hospital (with 24 hour emergency service)

    Name _____

    Address _____

    Telephone _____

Gas Company: Night _____

               Day _____

Electric Company: Night _____

                   Day _____

Plumber or Water Company: Night _____

                             Day _____